Older Women In Recovery

Sharing Experience, Strength And Hope

Helen Larimore, M.S., C.A.C.

Health Communications, Inc.
Deerfield Beach, Florida

Library of Congress Cataloging-in-Publication Data

Larimore, Helen
    Older women in recovery / by Helen Larimore.
        p.   cm.
    Includes bibliographical references.
    ISBN 1-55874-226-3
    1. Aged women — Alcohol use.   2. Alcoholics — Rehabilita-
    tion.   3. Aged women — Psychology.   4. Co-dependence
    (Psychology)   5. Aged women — Drug use.   6. Narcotic
    addicts — Rehabilitation. I. Title.
HV5138.L37   1992   92-4016
362.29'2'082—dc20   CIP

© 1992 Helen Larimore
ISBN 1-55874-226-3

Publisher: Health Communications, Inc.
              3201 S.W. 15th Street
              Deerfield Beach, Florida 33442-8190

Cover design by Barbara Bergman

Acknowledgments

To Judith Lin Eftekhar, my manuscript editor and my friend, for your mastery in systemizing and synthesizing, for your patience and plodding, for helping me to extract substance with style from the mountains of material these three years have accumulated and for your care to keep intact my words and intention, I give you thanks and respect. Your professional intelligence and flying fingers have contributed so very much to the completion of this project.

To that wonderful woman, senior editor Marie Stilkind, whose gentle wisdom and encouraging guidance have served as a backdrop for this book, thank you.

I also acknowledge and feel grateful to Corinne Kawecki, Nancy Katz and Linda Jenkins for your kindness and your contributions.

Contents

My Awakening

On my 45th birthday, I went to see my therapist for my weekly session. I was agitated. I squirmed. I pouted. "I hate getting old!" I finally blurted, unexpected tears of depression and self-pity suddenly spilling.

Eighteen years have passed since that day, but I remember well my therapist's mock serious countenance as she bent forward in her chair as if to share a secret. "Helen, you're not really old until you hit fifty-five, and besides," she declared confidentially, her own aging face framed by ink-rendered raven ringlets, "there's not a damned thing you can do about it!" We both chuckled, but I felt not the least bit reassured. My witty therapist's attempt to assuage the pain of my midlife crisis idled and died.

I left her office feeling resigned and resentful. It was September in the Midwest. Leaves turning, characteristically a sweet, sentimental season, the fall now seemed emblematic of the end of My Time. Looking back, I felt cheated of the 25 years of youth that I had endured in active alcoholism. This is the downside of believing in the disease concept, I soliloquized — feeling forever cheated by the illness.

Slogging home that afternoon in Chicago's early autumn heat, I persisted in pursuing the downward spiral. The negative self-talk droned on mercilessly. Didn't I deserve to remain young just a little longer? Hadn't I grappled successfully for the past five years with the challenges of recovery? Had I not galvanized my life to such an impressive extent that people were actually telling me how happy and amazed they were that I had cleaned up my act?

As I shuffled along, feeling increasingly downcast, I told myself that I had done my job. I had paid my dues. For a quarter of a century I had abused alcohol, marijuana, amphetamines and nicotine. I had been a round-the-clock, falling-down drunk, weighing 250 pounds, with sores of malnutrition covering my body and my hair falling out. And now I was totally abstinent. I had shed half my body weight. I was eating regular and nutritious meals and ingesting a daily arsenal of vitamins. I had become quite proficient in my hobby, candlemaking. I was working the 12 Steps of Alcoholics Anonymous. I had made steadfast strides in months of therapy, had talked about my early orphaning and the childhood sexual abuse. I was *clean*. I was doing everything possible to be honest and healthy. I was attempting assiduously to quit lying. Why, I had even stopped telling ethnic dialect jokes, which, I considered somewhat resentfully, had rendered great sacrifice to my popularity.

So where, I wondered, were the rewards? One day at a time I watched in terror as my face grew older, while my hair seemed to be greying by the minute. To make matters worse, I was searching desperately for someone to love me. Forlorn and despairing, I began to consider doing something that I despised in some other women, something that would have surged against all my sober values: I was about to start lying about my age!

As it happened, I never did tell that lie. What I did do was to begin addressing my own ageist attitudes, at the core of which were such deeply ingrained issues as "external referenting" and the "looking-good principle." Learning about my own ageism was as integral a part of my recovery and my serenity as any other aspect of my program, and equally as difficult to confront. Overcoming my internalized ageism also turned out to be the source of enormous and powerful freedom.

My thoughts about aging are quite different today. No longer do I believe that any time is ever lost in the darkness of our addiction, provided we eventually choose to live in recovery. In fact I believe that all of our lives' experiences, including the most trivial vagaries, are the building blocks we use in reconstructing our lives. Oh, sometimes I wish I had not been so totally zonked out on alcohol as not to experience fully the Beatles or Renata Tebaldi when I heard them live during my actively addicted time. And I certainly have regretted not being fully present and conscious on a train one wintry night some 40 years ago when, stumbling out of the bar car with a group of rowdy friends, I spotted Eleanor Roosevelt sitting alone, reading, her face partially covered by a dark veil.

But I consider it a miracle indeed even to have access to these recollections today. It is a miracle that I chose to survive at all after childhood traumas, broken limbs and alcohol, drug and food addiction. To say nothing of relationship addiction, which for years kept me in deep and familiar pain.

Neither do I now believe my erstwhile therapist's words, that I was entirely powerless over my aging. Aging, after all, is not merely a physical event. It is a process of the Self. Aging belongs to each of us. We can hide it in the shadows with shame, or we can sculpt it and turn it to the light. We can choose to hate it or to love it. Aging is a natural process of growing and learning, synthesizing and developing.

As human beings, we can learn from one another through our experiences in aging. That today's Western society disconnects youth from the aged, with injunctions to perform in prescribed ways according to chronological age regulation, with relegation to lower social and economic status as we advance in age, is both impolitic and unmerciful. Further, the limiting of intergenerational communication robs us of our wholeness and harnesses us to binding behaviors that do not profit either the young or the old.

What has happened to me in the years since my 45th birthday is what happens to anyone in recovery: life, with its peaks and valleys. What happened in my life was uniquely mine but not entirely atypical of many recovering women whose lives were interrupted by chemical addiction. At 46, I returned to graduate school to study the alcoholism sciences. To my delight, I found re-entering this structured scholastic environment after 25 years away to be intensely stimulating and ego-inflating. I flourished in the academic setting.

Around this time I became fascinated by the work of Virginia Satir. Many were the weekends I spent sitting in straight-back chairs in hotel conference rooms, hungrily observing the work of this brilliant woman who helped to heal the pain of thousands through her artful and creative work with dysfunctional families. She was my mentor-from-afar.

At the age of 50, outfitted with newly acquired credentials, I changed careers, from supervisor in a public aid office to alcoholism therapist in private practice. Immediately my client load became voluminous and unmanageable. Concurrently two local universities offered me adjunct professorial positions, both of which I eagerly accepted. My seminars on Women and Alcohol became popular, and I was in demand as a public speaker. I basked in the attention. My success gave me self-worth. I discovered that I was a creative and innovative teacher and my students loved me. In the early 1970s I had helped to establish a women's crisis line, one of the first in the country, which worked with women alcoholics and rape victims. Now I became a regular volunteer trainer, covering the areas of alcohol and drug abuse. I said yes to everyone.

Life had suddenly turned from lackluster to lively. And I was not lying about my age!

But by the time I turned 53, I had lost my right breast to cancer. Fortunately, I had detected the lump myself when it was still in an early stage, but it necessitated a surgical procedure called "modified radical mastectomy," a term representing one of the great oxymora of our time. The absence of node involvement, or *metastasis*, spared me the agony of chemotherapy, and for that I am ever grateful. The loss of my breast, however, was painful and reminiscent of my mother's death by breast cancer when I was nine. I now view the mastectomy as an important lesson, a catalyst to confronting my workaholism and ultimately to retracing and releasing my childhood pain.

The following year I shaved from my untenably busy schedule several working hours weekly, gathered up my savings and made a down payment on a 55-acre pocket of paradise in Wisconsin's unglaciated hills. For ten years now I have congratulated myself for taking that very smart risk. In my daily meditation I see that my returning for three days weekly to that Mother of us all, the earth, has helped to provide me with good health and increased longevity, and I have become filled with love. By reclaiming my rural roots, I am urged gently back to the euphoric memories of my childhood, to trees, birds and animals. My farm nestles me spiritually.

My cyclic return to the land was a prerequisité to my ability to involve myself in my recovery on a more profound and sustained level, by reawakening the lonely and abused child within me and thawing the frozen pain of my earlier years. This healing was neither planned nor easy. It continues as I continue — with acceptance, though not always easily flowing.

In 1981 I met Sharon Wegscheider-Cruse when *Another Chance* was gaining attention. I was intrigued by the non-sexist premise of her book, and I believed the fundamentals of her model to be in harmony with my own theories regarding recovery. Three years later, after attending countless seminars and workshops across the country, ostensibly to hone my therapeutic skills (oh, physician, heal thyself!), the pain of my ungrieved losses became intolerable, and I sought help from the Caron Institute. Soon I found myself sitting on top of a mountain in Pennsylvania, wailing and whaling away with a bataka bat. There I finally began to empty from my entrails the fermented pain of a troubled childhood. On a sunny afternoon in September, on my 57th birthday, bellowing and with tears flowing down my face, I found myself connecting with others, receiving. At last the healing of those long-neglected and most incisive wounds had begun.

Introduction

The winds of change are blowing across the Western mindscape, sweeping away outmoded beliefs about aging and scattering seeds of vital new truths. With every passing day comes a growing awareness of a collective creative spirit inherent among the elderly, a spirit both wise and useful to our culture. What began as the merest whisper during the second wave of flourishing feminism more than two decades ago, now resounds among the thousands of women who are involved in spiritually evolved recovery groups.

I speak of that level of consciousness that reaches across the chronology of years, winks at archaic concepts of physical limitations and makes extinct those dinosaurs of mythology kept alive by our culture's worn-out attitudes toward aging women. In the 1990s older women are riding an exhilarating new wave of energy released by the sound of our own voices. No longer content with silence, we are at last speaking. Our time has come.

For my part I feel ageless. I couldn't care less about what others think. I know what is appropriate for me. I work hard and gain great satisfaction from my work. I know where professional tennis is going, I follow figure-skating champions, I can dance a waltz or the Lambada. I subscribe to both the *Village Voice* and *Forbes* magazine. I have been to the rain forests in South America and have skied the Swiss Alps. I can speak knowledgeably about Monet and Mapplethorpe. Obviously, I can brag without feeling shame. No one can tell me I'm over the hill. I am *on top of the hill* and I see others joining me.

This book has grown out of my personal experience, both as a recovering older woman (I recently celebrated my 63rd birthday) and as a therapist for the past 15 years to women and men undergoing the arduous process of healing from alcohol and chemical dependence and from co-dependence. The research for this book became a golden legacy of the wonders of life as scores of older women opened their memory archives and generously shared stories of their personal pilgrimages. Like treasure troves, unearthed and laid open to the sun, these women shimmer and sparkle from one end of the earth to the other, from London to Mexico, from Maine to the Cayman Islands, from Los Angeles to Lucerne.

Some of these women have been my clients. Some are my friends. Many are those voices that have encouraged me through the years to write about our unique perspectives as older recovering women, about our special struggles and heroic healing. As one woman has said, we have survived the tornado and been through the briar patch. Therapists and addictionologists consider us, the aging addicted female, to be that population most resistant to the nonpharmaceutical therapeutic profferings of the health profession. They claim, in other words, that when it comes to mature women and recovery, rarely can it be done — but we are doing it!

The heartfelt purpose in writing this book is to deliver hope to those older women who may despair in their addiction or co-dependence, women who may find as their household maxims such mottos as, "What's the use?" "It's too late for me" and "What have I done to deserve this?" Increasing numbers of older women are in fact healing from the seething carbuncles of our disease, defining ourselves anew at any and every age. Women of earlier generations may have felt themselves to be "the forgotten ones," but older women today need no longer identify with this mournful label. Through our willingness and capacity to strive for awareness, those of us in recovery have dared to share our personal chronicles, which prove inspiring in their very revelations. We are changing ourselves. We are changing the fevered world we live in.

The decision to recover from our illness springs from a healthy desire for longevity, a determination to live life well before we die and to express ourselves once again in creative and intuitive ways. Regardless of our religious faith or our spiritual frame of reference, how we as individuals deal with our own mortality is demonstrated more clearly through how we live our lives than how we leave our lives.

My conversations with older women have convinced me absolutely of two truths: It is never too late to recover, and no matter what our age, we have all the time we need. This book presents myriad personal epics and varied viewpoints — including parts of my own story as well as my professional perspective — to synthesize the recovering women's primary concerns and to present the veritable toolbox of skills that they have found useful in their ongoing healing. No longer need we be isolated. By sharing in the process of retracing our experiences and reclaiming our long-neglected selves, by listening to and abetting each other in our individual strivings, we are learning that diversity means other than adversity, that it is our individuality as recovering women that intimately binds us together.

This book is about pain, humor, deliberation and purpose. It is an outgrowth of that loving cooperation and wisdom that only a group of older women in various stages of the recovery process can offer. It is written for those women who can remember *Pepper Young's Family,* Frances Perkins, the Dionne quintuplets, V-mail, cafe society, Vera Lynn, the Barrymores, speakeasies, margarine with a dot, Elsie Dinsmore, Margaret Sullivan, *Calling All Girls,* sailor dresses, Alice Adams, Alice Faye, Sweet Mama Stringbean, zoot suits, taffy pulls, bread lines, William Steig, box suppers, Armstrong Theater of the Air, Gegenschein, Rosie the Riveter, Russell Wright, *The White Cliffs of Dover,* Betty Boop, Burma Shave signs, hula-hoops, the sound of Winston Churchill's voice crackling through the airwaves, Fibber McGee and Molly, World War I, World War II, the Korean War and some peace in between.

This book is also written for the daughters and granddaughters of today's older women. To you I promise that what you may learn from the predicament and healing process of your predecessors will serve you in your own personal quest. It is a fact, too, that soon enough you will take your place in history as older women. My hope for you is that as you grow in your awareness of the hardships that your foremothers have endured, as well as the profound changes they have brought about, you may come to know that your own healthy attainments can make planetary changes in generations to come. As 76-year-old Frieda of Munich told me, the tearing down of the Berlin Wall was the result not so much of politics as it was of the lessons of peace taught by German widows of World Wars I and II, to their children and their grandchildren, now in their 30s and 40s. The women taught that separation and walls are not peacelike, that all the spoils of war are simply not worth the hurting generations and loss of connectedness to follow.

May we all gain a better sense of rootedness and belonging as we learn about other women who are not so unlike ourselves, after all, and come to recognize through them that physically, emotionally and spiritually vibrant living can be our reality at any age.

Interviews

My research began with a quest to speak with other older women who enjoy sobriety and recovery from dependence on alcohol and other chemicals and/or from co-dependence. My goal was to interview a minimum of 55 women, age 55 and older. In the beginning I encountered a great deal of defensiveness. It is an arduous task to pry open the long-locked doors of those closets that contain the family secrets and emotions, albeit some of those secrets are painfully burdensome to keep. Many women, even those ostensibly in recovery from co-dependence, would answer my questions with such statements as, "Of course, we're sick. My husband and I are both sick. We know that," but were reluctant to speak further about it.

As months passed and I continued interviewing, however, a kind of network unexpectedly evolved. Women contacted other women to tell them of my project. And to my joy and amazement, scores of extraordinary women came forward as word of the endeavor spread through 12-Step recovery circles across the country.

This was my first experience conducting research via the interview, and while I traveled extensively to meet with women during the three-year period, a good many interviews were conducted by telephone. Calls came from across the country, both from the daughters and granddaughters of older women and from older women themselves who were eager to be heard. Very quickly I recognized that the first lesson I needed to learn was that of patience and that in my own ageism I equated a slow response with a lack of mental agility. Often waiting long minutes while the woman at the other end of the line carefully gathered her thoughts and offered her innermost truths in response to my questions, I learned to slow down.

Ageism is subtle. I do not know at what point older women stopped sounding old-fashioned to me and began to sound profound.

I also learned to let go of concerns over my mounting telephone bills. In some cases the interview stretched out to three or four phone sessions over a period of months. Many women required extended periods of time to deliberate over my questions. Some made follow-up calls to revise their responses weeks or even months after completing the interview, in the interim having come to new realizations about themselves. As time went on, many checked back in with me to update their stories as their lives changed — as they became divorced, married or widowed, entered nursing homes or left them, progressed from wheelchairs to walkers, back to wheelchairs, sold their homes, moved, got sick, got better, won a lottery and so on.

It became apparent to me that the interview itself was providing my interview subjects with a sense of self-worth. Here was a connection to another person and a larger purpose, a repository of concern and care for the details of their lives. Here was an opportunity for the older woman to make a contribution to a better world for other aging women!

"All we really need to be happy is to feel we can still make a contribution," said Pat, a 58-year-old recovering alcoholic who not only served as an interview subject herself, but also referred to me at least a dozen others, including her own 76-year-old aunt, also in recovery.

Many of my subjects' names have been changed in this writing to comply with their request for anonymity. I have, however, stayed as closely to accuracy of detail as anonymity has allowed.

After interviewing 110 women, twice the number I had intended, I called a reluctant halt to the process. Even as I write this introduction, my telephone continues to ring. This week, nearly three years since I began the project, I received in the mail a diary from a 56-year-old woman dying of a cancer that began in her breast six years ago. The message she conveys is simple and courageous: "I live to the end in sobriety. I am ready."

I am grateful for this opportunity to examine the noble achievements of these venerable women and to rejoice with them in their transformations. To those among you who have felt you have not the mobility or economic resources to avail yourselves fully of the support services in your communities, I offer you the encouragement to reach out now. You are not alone. We are all connected. Other women somewhere near you share your hopes, your dreams, your strengths. Please take the courage to risk in some way and let them in.

Nature of the Interviews

I conducted my interviews starting with a basic list of 100 questions. These questions varied, according to each woman's individual circumstances and the nature of her recovery. An interview of a single woman recovering from alcoholism, for example, took a different tack from an interview of a mother of grown children who was recovering from co-dependence. The purpose of these "soft" interviews was not so much to gather statistically significant data as it was to search out the colors of confidence, the lively, vivid and sometimes mirthful vocal inflections and rich expressions of feelings that indicate to me that a woman has a firm foothold in living.

I include a sampling of my interview questions for the reader's information and elucidation. You may find it useful to pose these questions to yourself.

- What was one single event that brought you into recovery? What are you recovering from?

- How long have you been in recovery? How did you get here? Therapy? Twelve Steps? Treatment in hospital or program?

- What diseases have been fatal to your family predecessors? (Alcoholism, cancer, heart disease, diabetes, etc.) Is arthritis in your family of origin?

- Were you ever sexually abused? As a child? As an adult?

- If you are a recovering alcohol or drug addict, do you substitute addictions in your recovery? If so, how?

- When you were a young adult woman, did you have role models? Who was she (or they)? How was she special? Are you like that role model today?

- Is blood thicker than water?

- How are you planning to spend the next holiday? With whom?

- Who are the favorite men in your life? Who are the favorite women in your life?

- Were you ever paid for doing your family's laundry? How? What about the cooking and cleaning? Were you ever paid for that?

- Who was in charge of the bill-paying in your family of origin? Who is in charge of paying the bills in your family now? Whose money is it?

- Do you now have what you want? What you need? Do you feel what you have always wanted to feel? (Secure? Loved?)

- How do you describe the most painful period of your life? What were the years and the situation? Was that before or after your recovery began?

- When you were a little girl, were there old people in your life? Who were they? Did you like touching their skin?

- Were you ever conscious of being bored as a child? When were these times? Were you lonely? If so, did you know you were lonely?

- How was death dealt with in your family of origin? Did your family talk about it? Was it to be dreaded? Were you threatened with the heaven-or-hell concept? (If you are a good girl, you'll go to heaven; if you are a bad girl, you'll go to hell.)

Of course, if the "good" rules changed each day and you found you could *never* be good, did you then believe you'd go to Hell, anyway?

- Do you regularly watch television's sitcom *Golden Girls?* Why?

- What are your addictions?

- What do you still want to give or receive in your lifetime that you have not yet experienced?

- What is your family's most well-kept secret?

- What is the primary myth of your family of origin?

- Do you have a will? Is there an executor of your estate? How and why did you choose that person?

- What is your own most well-kept secret?

- Describe the happiest year(s) of your life.

- What is the earliest memory of your life? Who was with you?

- What are you feeling right now?

- Do you remember your dreams? If yes, are you the age you are now in your dreams? Are you a child? Are you any given age at all?

- What do you feel when you speak to others about the details of your childhood? With whom do you share these details?

- What is rightfully yours?

- Is there anything or anyone you would be willing to go to jail for?

- What does the word "advocate" mean to you?

- We often hear in recovery circles the phrase, "Whatever it takes . . ." What was the most difficult "whatever" for you, or what was the hardest thing to change in order for you to recover?

- Who cheated you in your childhood? Who cheated you in your adulthood? Who cheats you now?

- What are the sounds, smells and visual memories of your childhood that you remember? Which are the pleasant ones? The unpleasant ones?

- Do you feel safe?

- Who is the family storyteller in your family? If it is you, do you tell your family-of-origin stories in the presence of your spouse? If not, why not?

- Were there tasks you enjoyed doing as a child that you still enjoy performing? Which ones?

- Were there tasks you did not enjoy as a child that you do enjoy now?

- Do you have a daughter(s)? How do you want her to feel when she is your age? What do you want for her then? Do you have that now for yourself?

- Do you sometimes yearn to return to the area or home where you lived in your youth? Would you like to live there now? Was that in the country, village, town or city?

- What attitudes and behaviors in others are offensive to you relative to your aging process? (How do you feel, for instance, when someone tells you that you do not *look* your age?)

- What does "wise" or "wisdom" mean to you? Are you a wise woman?

- Would your family miss you if you were to die? Who exactly would miss you? For how long? Would anyone be relieved if you died? If so, who would that be?

- How do you want to die? When will that be, do you think? Did anyone die in the way you want to die? Who?

- What are you doing, generally, to prepare for the twenty-first century?

- What would you like to have happen when you finish this interview?

- What are you feeling right now?

- Who are your friends?

- Which of the following names are familiar to you?

Harriet Beecher Stowe
Shirley Chisholm
Aimee Semple McPherson
Betty Friedan
Emma Goldman
Margaret Mead
Rokelle Lerner
Marty Mann
Jeanette Rankin
Rosa Parks
Lois W.
Harriet Tubman
Sojourner Truth
Helen Aarli
Simone de Beauvoir
Virginia Satir
Robin Morgan
Martina Navratilova
Anna Moffo
Sweet Honey In The Rock
Rachel Carson

- How do you seek solace? Reading? What kind of reading? Music? What kind of music? Art? Exercise? Travel? Meditation?

CHAPTER ONE

Who We Are

We are the women America loves to hate. Women 55 years of age and older, we are the generation who ushered in today's baby boomers, those children who cut their teeth on Dr. Spock and *Leave It To Beaver*, the young adults who rode the roller-coaster ups and downs of the rebellious counterculture of the 1960s and of the 1980s' "greed decade." We are the mothers and grandmothers of those young people — more often young women, sometimes young men — now complaining to therapists and friends and whoever else will listen that they were presented with a surfeit of choices during their childhoods, that the plenitude of options, deficit of boundaries and other errors of our maternal ways are the source of their present-day distress. Punching pillows and screaming their anger in therapy groups, they are returning the blame and shame to their moms around the world. Interestingly, many of today's mothers and grandmothers participated in similar acts themselves as they blamed their own mothers in the decades of "momism" during the '50s and '60s!

We are wives and widows, teachers, secretaries, businesswomen, farmers, nurses, even therapists. We run the full socioeconomic gamut. Some of us are tree-huggers, dunes savers, flower children. Others are New England aristocrats, Native Americans, immigrants and expatriates from all parts of the world. We are overachievers, underachievers, nurturers, superwomen and supermoms. We are the power behind the throne and proud of it. Yet we are often depressed, sometimes without knowing it; often angry, sometimes without showing it. We give great love, yet feel unloved, depreciated and discounted.

Frequently we feel resentful of the subjugation we have suffered as women in our male-dominated culture. Yet we have done little to change our status. And why is this? *Because we have learned so well how to be "good women" in a society whose basic philosophy regarding women teaches co-dependence as normal and healthy.* We have been taught that it is our duty to take care of everyone else first and then, and only then, may we possibly be valued and loved. This message is reinforced in our every institution — in our families, in schools and churches, in the workplace and by the advertising and news media.

Our society as it functions today practices great denial of women's pain, commencing with the individual in her infancy, expanding to the family in her childhood development, radiating out into her community as an adult and terminating in her elderhood and death. As women, we take for granted our own positions, conditions and traditions, pain and all. Today, although catapulted cataclysmically through technological and industrial changes outside her home, a woman within her family is expected by herself and others to fulfill a role much the same as that of women generations ago. That is, she is to offer nurturance to her family, to act as the primary caregiver to her children and to uphold and protect her family's moral and spiritual values.

We see exhibited in a cross-section of older women those very characteristics that we find in our laundry lists of co-dependence and Adult Children of Alcoholics (ACoAs), in case-history profiles collected by intake workers in battered women's shelters, in the recorded documents of homeless women, in the rice-paper journals of the pampered and the privileged and in the memory writings of nursing-home drama groups.

Those "good women" among us who have dared to recognize our plight, who choose to recover from the painful bondage of chemical dependence and co-dependence, have discovered that our recovery can stir up a tempest of resentment among those around us who had grown so comfortable with the predictable script of our dysfunction. In recovery, when the older woman begins to set limits for herself in her caretaking role, she is viewed by other family members as abandoning her spouse and her children. No wonder, then, that this is a choice few of us make easily.

Ageism And Sexism: The Double Whammy

Women over the age of 55 are said to own the major portion of financial resources in this country, though perhaps largely by virtue of marriage or inheritance, considering that average wages earned by a working woman are low compared to a man. On the assumption that money means power, this fact alone ought to bestow upon us some semblance of recognition in our culture. Furthermore, older women have had a multitude of life experiences giving us possession of a degree of wisdom that is arguably greater than that of any other group of women or men in our society. We carry forth centuries-old traditions as healers and teachers. We have long lifetimes of practice in knowledgeably and competently addressing every conceivable crisis of living, from putting food on the family table during tough economic times, to working toward world peace.

Older women are probably more emotionally healthy than any other population group, and those of us in recovery from alcohol and chemical dependence and co-dependence are likely the healthiest. Older women are some of the most intuitive and creative spiritual beings around. And yet, despite all this, we are perceived by those around us — not to mention by ourselves — as that population group most powerless, most hopeless, most helpless, most diminished, most dreary, most uninteresting, most pitiful and more undesirable than any other group of either gender. We might just as well be invisible, a word that aptly describes how society views us — as white-haired, little old ladies, not even worth noticing.

This is truly a paradox. Why is it that older women are relegated to the bottom rung of the ladder? In pondering this mystery I can only conclude that our ill repute stems from a number of stereotypic notions about aging overall, and aging women in particular, that proliferate within our culture. Ours is an extraordinarily ageist society. We patronize the old, we ignore them or we deride them. Comics joke about old people and we are all supposed to laugh. Ageism may be the only "ism" left. Comics cannot joke in blackface anymore and sexism is becoming taboo, but old people are still fair game for ridicule. Further, advertisers avoid sponsoring television shows tilted toward over-50 viewers because they mistakenly believe that we are "locked in" for life in our consumer beliefs and cannot be convinced to buy their products. This will change, however, as our older population grows in number and health. Then we shall gradually lose our reputation for being inflexibly fixed.

Our society's skewed attitudes about aging begin with our very definition of the process. The sophisticated thesaurus that accompanies the word-processing software I use in writing this book offers these synonyms for the word *aging:* "decrepit, doddering, enfeebled, senile, shattered and exhibiting loss of mental faculties." It appears that my software may need consciousness-raising!

The Myths Of Older Women

Even a partial list of societal stereotypes about older women proves substantial:

Older women are physically unattractive. An older woman's natural aging process, from the wrinkles settling into her face to her slowing body movement, invites disdain. In our society, after all, a woman's appearance is expected to measure up to strict youthful standards. This is predominantly a woman's issue, for the stigma of aging truly belongs to women. Whatever is true of a woman in a sexist society is epitomized in the plight of older women, for they have lost what is viewed as women's privilege in our culture: physical attractiveness.

Older women suffer greatly at the whim of the media, from fashion magazines that ignore us to television sitcoms that ridicule us. The aging male in our society, however, is seen quite differently. Certainly, he does not need to bear with the "over-the-hill" or "no spring chicken" epithets tossed at women as they pass their child-bearing years. Men in our culture, in fact, tend to be viewed as increasingly mature, stately and dignified as they grow older. Unlike aging women, who are cast away as sexless beings, men continue throughout their lives to be held in high esteem as potential partners for women of all ages.

Society's response to a woman's aging can be debilitating. One woman I interviewed, a middle school teacher, explained to me why she retired early, at the age of 63. She related an incident that was both representative of society's cruelty and a factor in her decision to leave the career that had been her passion for three decades. One day in her classroom while she was mingling in the aisles with her students, she was touched on the arm by a preadolescent sitting at her desk. The young girl recoiled in mock horror and in a voice loud enough for all to hear said, "Oooh, yuk, *old skin!*"

Paradoxically older women who attempt to fit the mold run into a prejudicial wall. Even as we are urged to conceal our age cosmetically with makeup and hair dyes and even cosmetic surgery, we are criticized for doing so. "Well, she's on her third facelift," some may cattily whisper. We are not even supposed to be physically fit. On a segment of a daytime television talk show, a panel of female body-builders showed off their image of women as strong and muscular and suggested that working out with weights is something that all women can do. However, when a wom-an in the audience who was obviously in her sixties or seventies stood up and remarked that she really appreciat-ed the efforts of the young women onstage and wondered if bodybuilding could work for her, everyone laughed and no one on the panel answered her query. Obviously hu-miliated, the woman sat down.

For my own part, I happen to be very quick in body movement and possess great physical briskness. People tell me they would not dream that I am 63, so quickly do I move. The possibility that we are able to age with all of our physical agility intact is often lost in society's denial that older women continue to be productive and physically active beings in the world.

Older women are senile. A woman with grey hair or wrin-kles or other signs of aging is brain dead, this notion goes. An aging woman's brain has simply atrophied, wasted away, become paralyzed, vegetated or rotted, and she just can't reason or think anymore. Certainly we are all losing our memory. When a young woman forgets something, she is simply being human. When an older woman forgets something, however, she becomes someone to be worried about, patronized and belittled. Grandma — or Mom — forgot her hat today, so we conclude that she must be getting senile.

Quite to the contrary, the human brain can be remark-ably agile at any age. Scientific research has shown that mental activity actually perpetuates itself. The more we use our brain to think, solve problems and continue to use it, the less likely we shall "lose" it. What's more, re-searchers have hit upon an interesting angle to the aging person's apparent memory problems. Older people's long lives have filled their memory banks to the brim with material; hence, more time may be required to sift through it to recollect certain memory data!

This is not to negate or discount the reality of Alzheimer's and other tragic neurological diseases, but these disorders actually affect only a small percentage of the elderly.

Older women are deaf and blind. Haven't you heard? I have noticed that many younger people talk to me by yelling right into my ear. I have to inform them that I don't have a hearing problem and that they don't need to speak so loudly. People also believe that older women are blind, that we cannot walk down the street without stumbling over cracks in the sidewalk and falling. Essentially we are viewed as debilitated and weak. Boy Scouts used to be instructed to help us cross the street. They probably still are.

Older women are conservative and stodgy. Ridiculed as the Geritol generation, we are seen as being timid politically and personally possessing a "holier-than-thou" attitude that does not take real life into account. Contradicting this stereotypic notion, most older women in recovery have sustained in a lifetime of risk more physical violations — beatings, broken limbs, rape, incest — than they care to publicize. Some recovering alcoholics among us have truly walked on the wild side, having imbibed more alcohol in our day, having taken more hair-raising gambles and traveled more avenues of denigration and shame than we are willing to share.

Older women are overemotional and weak. "You're like a bunch of old ladies!" Macho men, among them many a dysfunctional father addressing his unfortunate sons, consider this a potent insult. Don't be an emotional weakling by feeling, the warped logic goes, by letting on that you are vulnerable and needy. Don't act like a helpless old lady.

Older women are angry. A slight variation on the previous stereotype, here we are viewed as overemotional in our expression of anger. We are grumpy and crotchety or outright enraged. This is a tricky issue because, the truth is, many older women *are* angry, a fact complicated by our culture's injunction against any woman expressing this emotion. Some older women carry mountains of unresolved, unexpressed anger from years gone by. But many of us are simply angry, and justifiably so, about things that affect us today, from sexism to the senselessness of war.

When a man says he is angry about injustice, people listen. But when a woman talks about inequities toward women in our society, she is quickly labeled an angry woman. This was noted by Allison, 67, a black housewife and second-grade teacher, peace movement activist in the 1960s and recovering co-dependent:

> I want to know why the fierce opinions of older women are frightening to others. We are in struggle. We are in combat. In war, people are combative and little can be said on such occasions that does not produce passion and ferocity. So it is with us. We are women who are every day in struggle to live. Doesn't anyone see us but us?

Older women — women in general — are deceitful. You can never trust a woman, goes this stereotype, because by nature she lies and cheats to get what she wants. Of course women are no more dishonest than men. But one area exists in which older women are forced to be truly mendacious: We often lie about our age.

Many women have good reason, they believe, to conceal their age. If physical beauty is the way a woman has felt power or authority in her youth, the loss of beauty signifies a much larger loss and is accompanied by great pain. The attempt to avoid this pain by hiding our true age, unfortunately, only makes matters worse. Age concealment is a pernicious process with numerous negative ramifications.

As I noted in the recounting of My Awakening, choosing to lie about my age would have placed me in direct conflict with the very principles of my 12-Step recovery. Lying about our age disturbs our balance and harmony, robs us of our honesty with our fellow beings, lowers our self-esteem and fills us with shame. And in the end, the lie is a losing battle, tantamount to ignoring the baby elephant in the living room. Inevitably the inevitable wins. Honesty, it turns out, is the best policy. Katherine told me:

> I took a big risk when I chose to begin to show my grey hair. I sensed both displeasure from my husband and rejection from some of my friends who considered I was betraying them by "going natural." My best friend told me with resentful inflection, "Everybody knows we graduated from college at the same time. Now they'll all know how old I am!" And a week after I was showing grey at my temples, my husband suggested uncharacteristically that I go for a week to a spa. He offered to pay for all of it as my 60th birthday present. But he was not able to tell me outright that he did not like my grey hair. That simple generous-looking gesture made me realize that conformity is a mandate, not only to teenagers, but to older folks who choose to remain in the looking-good lockup. I was appalled, hurt and angry. Now my hair is totally grey! It's my hair, and I love it.

Older women are useless. Our society considers women in general, but especially older women, not to be of much use. After all, we have lost the ability to bear children, so what worthwhile contribution could we possibly make? Much is heard in the news these days about "throwaway" children who are found living on the streets because they come from neglectful, abusive families. The term "throwaways" equally applies to a growing number of older women who, no longer being the keeper of the flame, the manager of the household or the mother of young children, often divorced or widowed, have been forgotten by their families and communities. Some of these women live in the street and are labeled bag ladies. Others, hidden away in society's darkest corners, are indeed unidentified throwaways.

"Widowed women past their childbearing age have almost no chance of remarriage, while widowed men of any
age soon marry women significantly younger than themselves," note Lois Grau and Ida Susser in their book,
Women In The Later Years. "Older men are much more likely
to receive social and personal support in traditional families because of their high status as males, economic independence and likelihood of being married and having a
spouse to provide care. Older women fall short of men on
[all of these accounts] and their situation, inside or outside
of the family, is more likely to decline with the frailties
brought about by old age."

Gerontophobia

These attitudes are due in part to *gerontophobia,* the fear
and hatred of old age. Gerontophobia is societal terror, a
condition caused in part by the industrialization of the
early twentieth century and the multiple migrations from
rural to urban living. This upheaval and the piling together
of masses of people in environments of concrete and
street signs have served over a period of a half century to
cut children off from the changing of earth seasons and
the birth and death cycle of animals and plant life as part
of the natural order of our universe. Hence, children in
our modern culture fail to experience the passing of life
into death as natural for all living species. Consequently
they view the death of a grandparent, for example, as
separate and isolated from other life events.

Parents who are not accustomed to feeling their feelings
do not know how to talk about death to their children.
They do not like to think about death because they fear it
themselves. And their children, watching the murders and
horror on television as their only reference to death, then
frequently view death as gruesome, dolorous, even macabre. If sweet Grandma's death means to them that she is
turning into a vampire or a zombie, doomed to walk forever among the gravestones, then certainly death is not
welcomed as a subject of conversation.

Forty percent of the women I interviewed who were mothers felt that their families would not feel pain for very long if they were to die. And most social service agencies, they believe, would just as soon they'd go away.

Mixed Messages

At the very same time society tells older women to be and look young, paradoxically we are not supposed to *act* young. We are expected to exhibit certain behaviors befitting our advanced age. A humiliating experience of my own drove this point home:

I have always been a basketball enthusiast, having played it in high school and during my undergraduate years at the University of Illinois. Over the years, my enthusiasm in the game waned as my life led me in other directions. Then a couple of years ago I decided to attend a basketball game of my alma mater. I went alone. It was an exceptionally thrilling game with well-matched teams. In my excitement I stood up and cheered when my dear *Fighting Illini* scored. Everyone in my bleacher row was standing, yelling and cheering. It was a moment of total absorption.

Suddenly, someone behind me yelled, "Sit down, Grandma, and act your age!" Surprised, I turned around, at first unaware that the young man, seated, was addressing me. Then I noticed that everyone was staring at me. Immediately I felt humiliated and embarrassed. Old messages kicked in: I had done something wrong. I had been inappropriate. I had crossed a forbidden boundary. As I sat down, I could feel my face grow hot, my shoulders slump forward. My heart pounded as the shame set in.

It was as if I were eight years old again, playing on the floor with my little three- and four-year-old cousins and being blamed for their fighting and crying. I could hear my father's voice, booming through the 50-some years of silence since his death, "Get up off that floor and act your age!"

Now, what is positive about this narrative is I did know how to take care of myself. Before I left the gymnasium that night, I telephoned a friend, a sister recoverer, who joined me at a local coffeehouse for tea and empathy. There, over steaming mugs of chamomile tea (mine with a twist of lemon grass), my friend told me I was a powerful and courageous woman for not leaving the game until it was over. She reminded me that I certainly was a lovable and worthy creature in the world. I went home feeling just fine.

Our culture holds older women in disdain, yet clings to a lovely ideal of us as passive, pale and permanented. Even clothing styles have social acceptability according to age. Appropriate clothing for "mature" women is relegated to separate sections in department stores. We shall not find the orange leather miniskirt hanging there, waiting for the over-55 woman to try it on. And if she were to show up at her bridge club wearing one, she would likely be inviting social censure.

Society wants to see its older women as sweet and smiling, bespectacled, tied into a flowery apron and pulling a hot apple pie fresh from the oven, all the while slightly senile and essentially powerless. In our all-or-nothing society those aging women who are not compatible with that vision are frequently viewed as controlling, rigid, angry and mean.

Challenging The Myths

As older women we need to challenge our culture's myths. We must take care of ourselves both as individuals and as colleagues engaged in mutual struggle. Isolation from one another and competition among ourselves needs to end. We must look within ourselves at the barriers we have constructed that have kept us apart. Competition for men's favors has kept us apart; learned impatience with other women has kept us apart; prejudicial attitudes toward widows, divorced women and single women have kept us apart; all sorts of cunning, baffling and powerful internalized beliefs have kept us apart. I myself have been their victim.

For most of my life, even as I aged, I avoided contact with older people as much as possible, mostly because of my own fear of aging. Demythologizing society's definition of women's role becomes much more real and exciting as increasing numbers of older women enter the process of recovery, resolute in facing their addictions. Simply stating that we oppose the perpetuation of the myth, however, is not enough. We must earn credibility as role models by healing ourselves and then becoming unified in our centeredness and in our stance.

Every recovering older woman bears the onus of having to address her own biases resulting from what amounts to our society's addiction to youth. "Magical" facial creams, hair dyes, the billion-dollar business of plastic surgery, from facelifts to liposuction — the parade of lobbyists for keeping women eternally youthful is endless. The profit motive in our culture has long had a major influence in the shaping of women's lives through advertising. And then there's the massive matter of making sure we continue to be the "good women" the myth would have us be.

Leading this charge is the world of modern medicine. Prescription drugs — the tranquilizers, both major and minor, antidepressants, amphetamines and who-knows-what-else — are formulated either to anesthetize or to stimulate, whatever it takes to alter our attitudes. Medications do, of course, have their place in the treatment of chemical imbalance, but they are not a legitimate substitute for the therapeutic process. Twice as many women as men nationwide seek professional treatment for depression and emotional pain, and women are the major consumers of prescription drugs. The classic explanation is that women are inherently weak, congenitally unstable and hysterical. No mention is made of the possibility that we have simply *had it* with society's expectations. Not that we have made this message clear. Indeed, in the last half century, such deadly drugs as Thorazine and Xanax, lobotomies and the indiscriminate use of shock treatment have left many women literally sedated for life.

Toni, 67, a recovering alcoholic and co-dependent, complained vigorously, "We are not allowed to express our anger. We are expected to toe the line, let go without making waves, forgive and forget, give, give and give some more. But never complaining, for to do so is unladylike."

In societies around the world, a man's needs are inevitably interpreted as more important than a woman's. Generally, it is not permissible that a woman question, let alone challenge, male privilege.

As writer and philosopher Simone de Beauvoir in her book *The Second Sex,* so acutely observed:

> Woman is doomed to immorality because for her to be moral would mean that she must incarnate a being of superhuman qualities: the "virtuous woman of Proverbs," the "perfect mother," the "honest woman," and so on. Let her but think, dream, sleep, desire, breathe without permission and she betrays the masculine ideal.

Recovery And The Older Woman

Fortunately it is not particularly unique to find women over 55 who are in recovery from alcohol and/or other chemical dependence, which is defined as that state of being wherein an individual is physiologically or psychologically dependent upon these drugs. A great many older women are in such recovery. Some have been sober since 1935, when Alcoholics Anonymous (AA) was founded, although very few women joined that fellowship in its early years, as it was generally believed at the time that women did not have alcoholism. In the decades since, an increasing number of women have come out of their pantries and closets, to become visible and join AA.

Recovery begins essentially by quitting, not simply giving up, an addiction. It is not a process of sacrifice. We simply stop doing something that is killing us. A woman in recovery from alcoholism or chemical dependence can be a woman who attends AA meetings and who works the 12 Steps; she may have been in an inpatient treatment program for alcoholism or drug dependence. She may also be working a program for another addiction or for an eating disorder. She may or may not be in therapy.

In some cases she may have defined herself as alcoholic or drug dependent and may be in a recovery program of her own design. One woman I interviewed told me that she had stopped drinking six years ago at the age of 52 solely through reading various materials that she ordered through the mail. She engages in no adjunctive self-help or therapy. A rural woman who does not drive a car, she does much of her living by mail order.

What *is* unique today in the area of recovery, hearteningly, is the dramatically increasing numbers of older women who are finding the courage to heal from co-dependence. Interestingly many older women enter co-dependence recovery through the back door of alcoholism or chemical dependence, having been pushed to the edge by society's disdain toward her disease. Social and family stigmatism of female alcoholics, though, has been great and continues to proliferate destructively across our nation.

To admit that one's wife, mother, sister or daughter is an alcoholic is to admit a dark and well-kept secret. In this, as in many other aspects of her life, an older woman's problems are magnified. If a budding young alcoholic woman in her 30s encounters unfriendliness and irritation among her peers, certainly the older alcoholic woman will meet with hostility. A young alcoholic woman is considered disgraceful and inadequate in her roles as wife and mother, but the older alcoholic woman signals a gaping sense of shame, uselessness and burden. While neither finds herself in an enviable position, both threatening society's image of the "good" mother and wife, the older woman must also deal with increasing concerns about her physical health, fears of financial insecurity, loneliness and death.

On the positive side, the older woman in recovery from addiction discovers vast inner resources. Many of the older women I interviewed told me their ability to withstand ongoing pain and cope with crisis has been greatly strengthened through their recovery from chemical addiction. In learning to trust their own physical and emotional healing process they have become autonomous, serene beings — wise, resourceful and fearless. These very characteristics serve them well in taking on the further challenge of facing issues of co-dependence. We realize that if we are not too old to fight addiction in ourselves, we are not too old to work for what we want and need in all areas of our lives.

Co-dependence Defined

"A pattern of painful dependence on compulsive behaviors and on approval from others in an attempt to find safety, self-worth and identity. Recovery is possible." Thus was co-dependence defined and hope proffered during the first National Conference on Co-dependency in 1989. The "doormat syndrome," as co-dependence has also been described, is played out in obsessive caretaking and people-pleasing to the ultimate detriment of all involved.

Co-dependence is, in essence, a painful addiction to relationships. All chemically dependent women are co-dependent. Co-dependence is a way of life with themes and patterns in the ways we relate to others. Someone has said that it is a lifestyle with low self-esteem at the core. Among the symptoms are . . .

- difficulties with intimate relationships
- difficulty trusting
- all-or-nothing judgments
- grandiosity
- fear of abandonment and need for abandonment
- the need to seek out people to take care of, to "fix" and to make them dependent upon us
- the need to control oneself as well as others.

A more complete list largely mirrors the list of characteristics of Adult Children of Alcoholics (ACoAs), who as a group were one of the first to be clinically observed from a psychological perspective. In fact, the symptoms of children exposed to a wide variety of other dysfunctions

in their families of origin are very similar to those of
ACoAs, and we shall concern ourselves with these symptoms throughout this book.

Of course, all families in any sexist society have some
degree of dysfunction. On the continuum between well-
ness and illness, the dysfunction that crosses over the
median mark toward greater illness is found more frequently in families of alcoholism or other chemical dependence, as well as in families with single, divorced or
widowed parents, fatherless families, families in which
there is physical violence, families in which a parent is a
rageaholic and families demonstrating rigid religiosity or
other obvious extremes.

The dysfunctional, or toxic, family fails to work in ways
that are satisfying, that give pleasure or happiness to its
members. Instead, it is based on mistrust, doubt, shame,
guilt, blaming, a sense of inferiority, isolation and frozen
roles. Absent are emotional, physical and verbal intimacy.
Members' moral and social values are conflicting and confusing. Often there exists sexual conflict. Disciplining of
the children is frequently inconsistent. The family
members feel isolated from each other and lack a sense of
belonging, both in their families and in the larger world.
They may feel lost, stagnant and hopeless.

In order to cope with such a family as children we formed
co-dependent beliefs and behaviors that served us well in
getting what we needed to survive. When we later discover
that these old skills no longer work for us, but work against
us, we begin to make choices to recover from the ills sustained in the fracas and fray of our family's dysfunction.
This recognition often proves difficult for many older
women because, as stated earlier, ours is a society that
teaches women that co-dependence is normal and healthy.

The older woman recovering from co-dependence is, in
effect, relinquishing her "main job" in life. She must re-
nounce many of those fundamentals handed down to her
in her childhood, tenets that she believed she had to hold
dear in order to be a good wife, mother and grandmother,
a good woman overall. She must admit, further, that some

of her standards and methods of parenting did not work well and indeed may have inflicted pain. She must admit that traditional parenting and good intentions were not enough. She must admit that what was deemed virtue may have been quite flawed. In short she may have to conclude that much of what she accomplished in her long years of parenting and grandparenting was either inappropriate or harmful in some way to her family. How painful this is!

It is not that older women were "bad" mothers. Most of them did the best they knew how. It is at this juncture, however, that we become irresponsible if we stop with that simple recognition. We owe it to ourselves and to others to ferret out the exact nature of our disease and to heal from it. Healing means making changes. Life will never be altogether easy but recovery can bring new resilience in the face of any challenge.

Irene, 57, is a perfect example of this. The mother of four adult children and a courtroom stenographer for 21 years, she is in recovery from co-dependence and is the widow of an unrecovered alcoholic:

> In the last five years our family has been hit hard by everything from my daughter-in-law falling off a ladder and breaking her back to my granddaughter being diagnosed with leukemia. I believe I would have died if I had not had my Al-Anon friends and my women's therapy group to talk with. Together, there's not much we haven't dealt with. Just being able to share my problems has made me feel less alone and afraid. The best thing is that I am changing. I don't stay with the problem night and day like I used to for years, unable to sleep or work because I obsessed on the family so much. Even in the midst of all the torment, I find peace now, knowing there's not a lot I can do to change anything but myself and my attitude.

The Responsibility To Recover

Recovery from alcoholism and other addictions is highly commendable, but in the continued presence of co-dependence, it is not enough. Were I to draw a line between my own recovery from alcoholism and my recovery from co-dependence and dysfunctional living, that line would mark the place where I began to reclaim my *emotional sobriety.*

Earnie Larsen talks about this in his book *Stage Two Recovery.* When we progress from the self-help group AA to the self-help group Co-dependents Anonymous (CODA), we go from dealing with our addiction to dealing with our affliction. We are dealing with part two of what is our double-craziness.

As older women it is our mature responsibility to recover from co-dependence, not only to improve our own lives, but to pave the way for healthier, happier lives for generations of women to follow. We simply must offer them something better than what we were taught was the fate of being born female.

There are, incidentally, critics of the co-dependency movement who look askance at the very concept of co-dependence as an illness, let alone the need for recovery from it. What we call co-dependence, they say, is simply the nature of people everywhere, that families are all going to have dysfunction. That is what normal is, they say.

But normal is not necessarily healthy. Should we need proof, let us look at what is happening in our world. We see a lessening of regard for the preciousness of human life. We condone war rather than promote peace. Our impoverished neighborhoods — with increasing numbers of homeless people, escalating statistics of murders and rapes, insufficient incomes, poor diet and health, mounting addictions, that is, neighborhoods suffering abysmal neglect by our country's domestic policymakers — are painful illustrations of the "normalcy" of the abominable. People who allow these conditions to arise and continue all come from some place of dysfunction!

As responsible citizens, we must actively counter resignation to such an atrocious norm. Co-dependent women who see co-dependence all around us must summon the courage to say, "The buck stops here." We cannot change the past, we cannot rear our children anew, but we can change ourselves and become the models of new attitudes and new behaviors.

The older woman's responsibility to recover also involves a refusal to perpetuate society's lies with respect to her aging process. In so doing, unfortunately, she may risk condemnation. Yes, we have come a long way, baby, but if we are told again and again in our recovery that our self-esteem must be heightened if we are to be healthy and autonomous, then addressing the aging issue becomes essential. We must be honest and love our age, love our aging being, love our aging bodies. We simply must embrace reality.

Observed Joan, a woman of wit and beauty in her early 70s, living in Miami Beach, Florida, and in recovery from co-dependence:

> I see many co-dependent women obsessing on their appearance, their weight, their fear of losing their husbands' love. This sabotages their recovery process. When it is no longer safe to have another facelift, when the body-tucks no longer work and the skin ruptures, and after the silicone breasts have fallen around their waists and caused irreparable damage, these women finally have to get real. Then they plunge into deep depression. They just don't know how to act, being older. This isolates them socially and denies them access to many segments of society because in their years of denial they haven't learned how to grow older gracefully.
>
> I used to do that whole number, too, until I found out that bleaching my hair wasn't going to keep my husband at home if he didn't want to be there. Not long after that I began to get serious about my program and my life. I stopped smoking when I was 68. Now I really am okay, no matter who's around. My husband died last year, and I get lonely sometimes but I know that's normal, too. I don't think about my own death too much. I'm just grateful I have today.

We can deal with our dysfunction no matter what our age. We are never too old to change. The only requirements are desire and willingness. We may try to avoid making changes, try to deny the need for them. But consider this: One thing we cannot avoid, especially as older women, is our continued aging. The best we can do is to choose the manner in which we approach it. We can view it with dread or we can fashion it while our sun still shines. We can improve our lives starting right now. It is never too late.

Last year I attended a workshop on co-dependence given for training counselors. The facilitator, a highly skilled therapist and undisputed expert in our field, used workshop participants in a psychodramatic demonstration to portray experientially the dynamics of family dysfunction. She constructed a family sculpture in which the grandfather, along with his son-in-law, was depicted as a practicing alcoholic. The generational chain of addiction and co-dependence was quickly observable. The grandmother was directed to stand behind her husband, supporting his "drinking elbow" as he leaned against her. Both were instructed to stand behind the others in this three-generation family portrait.

As the workshop progressed, we were shown how the interaction among the other family members would change if the son-in-law were to enter into alcoholism treatment. Positive results soon became evident as communication opened up among the members of the second and third (youngest) generation. When I raised my hand and asked what would shift in the family unit if Grandpa were to go to Alcoholics Anonymous, the audience laughed loudly and the workshop convenor replied, "Nothing."

It was in that moment, seeing in living color this frozen cameo of co-dependence, that I recognized in the treatment community an attitude of disinterest toward older people, and specifically older women. There was Grandma up on that stage, tractable and tame, standing behind her "man," literally holding him up. She was barely visible. Why, something certainly *would* change, I thought, somewhat chagrined at seeing such obvious societal carelessness. Grandma would lose her job if Grandpa got sober!

This was hardly an authentic description of the aging co-dependent who spawned the generation of baby boomers who today are re-creating yet another remake of Grandpa.

Then who is she, if not the scrawny martyr who whines, unnoticed and forgotten, behind Grandpa? Certainly, it was not always thus. Once she was the force that pulled the children out of bed for school, pushed her spouse to work, staved off bill collectors, created culinary magic from morsels and finally went out of the house to work to clothe her family and pay the rent. She was the one who cleaned the splattered toilet of her husband's vomit so she could rinse their children's soiled diapers there. She was the one who lied for him when he was too sick from alcohol to go to work. And she was the one who cried for him when he begged her forgiveness for all the broken promises and faded dreams. And she kept taking him back. Again and again.

Perhaps it was not like that. Perhaps Grandma drank alcohol right alongside her husband. It is possible she was also an alcoholic, equally adept at making and breaking promises, a co-conspirator of manipulation and brutality. It is possible that *she*, in quite a different family sculpture, is the identified patient, the alcoholic mother whose eight-year-old daughter came home with a playmate after school one wintry afternoon 64 years ago to find her leaning, nude and unconscious, against the radiator in an upstairs bathroom, empty wine bottle clenched in her hand. Perhaps she still carries the psychic scars and the shame-shrouded secret fear that these girls, now in adulthood, still remember with horror the sight and smell of her seared skin clinging to the radiator as they pulled her body away from it.

Such fears and secrets are not easy to live with, but neither are they unusual in the annals of recovering older women.

CHAPTER TWO

The Caretaker

"I have been fixing my family for so long that if I leave them now, I'll feel like I am letting them down," said Barbara. "They *need* me."

Barbara's sentiments have been echoed by many of my women clients in co-dependent recovery as well as by numerous others interviewed for this book. These feelings are a sure signal of what is called caretaking, the primary dysfunctional role played by female co-dependents.

In the classic enmeshment of the addicted, dysfunctional family, the family members all need one another to take care of them in ways that prevent them from having to do it themselves. An example often used is that of the woman who calls in sick for her hung-over husband the morning after so that his employer will not suspect that he is an alcoholic. But there is also the big brother who does little brother's homework so that he doesn't flunk out of school. And the eldest daughter who silently surrenders to her father's incestuous advances to prevent her parents' fighting about their own sexual conflicts.

By meeting the needs of others, caretakers aim ultimately, albeit indirectly, to have their own needs met. "It is my responsibility to take care of others," the caretaker believes. "In exchange for this, they will have to take care of me." Unfortunately she does not communicate her needs and expectations, and therefore the results do not balance out as neatly as she imagines that they will. More often than not, the caretaker's needs are benignly ignored or denied outright. She gives and gives but rarely receives in return.

So why would anyone choose to be a caretaker? Because women in our society, especially older women, have traditionally been taught that what is tantamount to co-dependency is their required role in life. Society has long held and still holds to the belief that women's reproductive organs oblige them to serve as sole nurturers and as nurturers solely. Women, not men, are charged with emotional support and nurture. Giving, not receiving, is a woman's *raison d'etre*. Caretaking in our sick society, then, is considered normal and healthy behavior.

In some ways, I used to think that I was fortunate in having been orphaned at the age of nine. While I was lonely and lacked nurture, I certainly was not burdened with the responsibility of taking care of my parents when I grew into adulthood, as so many of my friends had learned as a part of their parents' expectation of them and who later found themselves living out this life-long edict, struggling painfully with aging parents. To the contrary, as a child I felt I did not serve any useful purpose. I felt myself to be in the way, simply no good to anyone. "Stay out of the way" was the message I received generally from my relatives.

I was in college when I first observed a behavior in young women that helped them get what they wanted. If ever I was a fast learner, in this area I absolutely excelled. Overnight, I learned how *to take care of* roommates, boyfriends, professors, housemothers, employers, librarians, anyone and everyone. It was a miracle! To think that I could get what I wanted simply by pleasing others!

Never mind that I had to drink beer to excess to forget my pain. Never mind that I had to lose that part of Topsy who was a part of me, that wild and woolly free-spirited orphan from Harriet Beecher Stowe's *Uncle Tom's Cabin*, that savage child who answered to no one and who, when asked who raised her, answered, "Nobody. I just growed!" The rewards of my college caretaking were just too great to worry about the drawbacks. The rewards were, in a word, finally belonging. At last I had a place in the world, a role to play, a reason to be. And soon I was good at it!

Caretaker Of Children

Where does caregiving end and caretaking begin? Child care has traditionally been women's work. *Ozzie and Harriet, Father Knows Best* and other popular television programs of the 1950s depicted the ideal American family: Father went off to work and Mother stayed home with a house full of kids and a sudsy sinkful of dishes. Today's mothers, of course, often report to full-time paying jobs, too, as well as maintaining primary responsibility for the children and the housework, adding up to two full-time occupations instead of one.

Caregiving women are permitted to seek nurture in one place — from other women — but only on the condition that they pass on this energy, this commodity that is believed to be unending in its quantity, to their families. Women's role as primary nurturer is not only an incredibly difficult and demanding one, but it has contributed to deleterious and enduring competition among women, not just for the favors of men, but, more recently, for a place beside men in the corporate world.

Mothers are held responsible for their children's successes. Mothers are homework enforcers and scholastic cheerleaders, social secretaries for their children's wholesome social lives and bestowers of ethical and spiritual guidance. One payoff to caretaking women, and a loss to their children, is in their feeling justified in pridefully taking credit for their children's every accomplishment, from Johnny's first steps six months before the neighbors' children, to Kathy's acceptance into medical school.

Conversely "bad mothers" are blamed for all of their children's problems, not only during their childhoods, but for the rest of their lives. Sigmund Freud pointed to Mom's failure to breast-feed or to her harsh toilet training as origins of psychiatric pathology. Mothers are also blamed for social ills and criminal behavior. If only his mother had paid more attention to him when he was a kid, maybe Tom would not have become a serial murderer. When we refer to society's undesirables, after all, we refer to them as "sons of bitches."

A caretaking mother is an overburdened mother even after the children have grown up and moved out, for then there are in many cases the grandchildren to care for. In families living in poverty, especially in those escalating numbers of households headed by single mothers, it is commonly understood that the grandmother will rear her grandchildren while their mother is away at work or school. So inculcated has this become in African-American culture that hardly anyone notices the tired and selfless grandmother taking care of generation after generation of young people.

This is not to suggest that grandmothers do not enjoy caring for their grandchildren, some even feeling vibrant and regenerated by their continued contact with children. However, as 66-year-old Ginny, a widow in Utah who has taken care of her grandchildren since her son's divorce, lamented:

> I love my four grandchildren, but I just never have had time to sit down. I always thought I would. Now, since my daughter-in-law left, I don't know when I'll ever be able to sit down.

Ginny's opportunity to "sit down" is, as she views it, completely contingent upon her son's remarrying. Unless and until that happens she considers it her duty as the woman of the household to rear her grandchildren.

Many older women devote their dwindling energies to their grandchildren out of guilt for having done things "wrong" the first time around with their own children. They worry that they will fail again, this time as surrogate mothers. They continue to give of their time and energies, resentful and exhausted though they may become. And if they choose not to keep giving, they risk rejection. Says Carol, 57, mother of six:

> I swear it was the hardest choice I ever had to make when my daughter asked to move in with us with her two children under three years after her alcoholic husband disappeared, but I knew if I had to change one more diaper or deal with one more bout of colic in the night or take one more of my precious weekends to give child care, I'd be dead myself. So I said no. Now my daughter barely talks to me. My husband and I send her money monthly to help her out and she accepts it. But she is very hurt and angry. She believes she still has a right to live here, that as her parents we still owe her a place to come to with her children. Now, that is a message we gave her when we were still very sick in our caretaking and didn't want her ever to leave us. Those messages are hard to change after children grow up. We realize now that those old family values were not healthy for us or for our children, after all.

Caretaker Of Men

"He's going to retire in two years," said Linda, 61. "I dread it. What am I going to do? I'd rather die than be cooped up having to take care of him! I'll go crazy if I have to do that!"

"He just won't pick up a thing," said June, a 72-year-old woman in AA. She is partially paralyzed by a stroke, yet her husband, Joe, refuses to help with cooking and cleaning. "He was born in a generation which believes the wife does all the housework and for a man to do it is sissy. He says it's *sissy*."

Confessed Constance, 58, in co-dependent recovery, married to a recovering alcoholic, "I hate to say it, but I hope he dies before I do. I have never had a life of my own. I wanted to get away from him when he was drinking but I had always read that women live longer than men. So I stayed with him. Besides, I had no skills outside the home to make a living for myself and my three kids or I would have been gone 30 years ago. Now I'm not so sure. I'm the one who is sick and tired of being sick and tired. He seems to be fine. What if I have lived all my life waiting for my rewards and he outlives me?"

Women are vested with responsibility for their men. From an early age, women have been taught to act as aides to men, as housekeepers, secretaries, helpmates to their careers, assuagers of their pain, boosters of their egos, ofttimes the quiet power behind the kingly throne.

Recently on a cruise where my sister and I meet every year for our annual family reunion of two, we shared dinner with an aging childless couple, Hans and Laura, from Denmark. One night, after several evenings of dining together as well as sharing some of the personal details of our lives, I spoke of my writing this book. When I began to describe its contents and general purpose, Hans, a decorous and conservative clergyman, shrugged and interjected that it all sounded to him like "women's lib." A dialogue ensued in which we discussed the right of women to be ordained as ministers, currently a heated issue in their social priestly circles. Laura proclaimed her abhorrence at such an idea, declaring that she simply could not imagine why any woman would want to become a minister, that there was plenty of other work to be done in the church, the ministry was men's work. She herself, she said, would never want to be married by a woman minister.

I left the dinner table that night wondering if women will ever stop swallowing the line that inferior is superior. For most of her life Laura had worked as a volunteer in their church, performing auxiliary and lowly tasks. Meanwhile, her ordained spouse traveled to many exotic lands as a church administrator. Her duties, although characterized ostensibly as humble and worthy "church work," were nevertheless frequently onerous, backbreaking and generally scabrous. She appeared to me to be merely an aging satellite to a spouse who was still a shining star in their community. But a paradox cannot be disregarded: On this ship floating across the Caribbean Laura made all the decisions regarding her and her spouse's living and eating arrangements. She also chided him in small ways — his use of the wrong dinner fork, his inaccuracy of detail in recounting the day's events. In such small ways did she assume some semblance of power.

In marriage women are expected to uphold the traditional vows, come hell or high water . . . for richer or for poorer, in sickness and in health, till death do us part. The onus of a failed marriage often falls upon the woman, who is viewed as having failed to give adequate nurturance or to be attractive enough to keep her man at home. The message to women long has been: Make sure your marriage stays together — regardless. In some cases, as in that of marriage to an alcoholic, this means regardless of how much depredation, loss of dignity and integrity she may suffer. If the woman herself has a drinking problem, she is surely doomed to failure. Noted Cindy, 59, who is of Mexican extraction:

> My culture believes in family loyalty and male dominance. Our women's fiercest pride is in taking care of our men. Since this is true, and the stigma of women's drunkenness is so very harsh in our culture, it is practically impossible for a woman to recover from alcoholism. She hides her drinking in the first place and then has to hide her recovery as well.

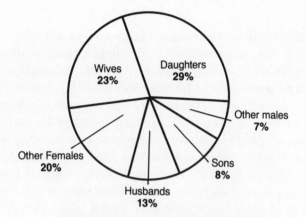

Who Takes Care of the Elderly?
More than 2 million people provide unpaid assistance
to elderly people living outside of nursing homes
or institutions. Almost three-fourths of the
caregivers live with the persons receiving the care.

Society assumes that women are "naturals" as in-house
nurses, be the patient mildly or deathly ill. If a household
has in it an older person who is chronically ill, it is very
likely that this person is male and that his wife is his
primary caregiver. He quite possibly has been, or still is,
an active alcoholic who suffers from disabling alcohol-
related diseases.

If his spouse is also unwell, her needs are often considered secondary to those of her husband, who wants no
one but her to care for him. If her husband is healthy, an
ill, aging woman will generally be placed in a nursing
home or in sheltered care. The man in her life does not
volunteer to take care of her, neither is he expected to.
Some women told me they were fearful that their husbands would leave them if they displayed signs of physical
illness. "My husband can't stand being around sick people,"
said 75-year-old Edna, who suffers silently with a spastic
colon and arthritis in her hands.

The recovering aging woman who is her spouse's primary caregiver very often is isolated and lonely. If she had
been attending AA or Al-Anon meetings, she now no
longer does so because of her husband's need for round-

the-clock care. Making matters worse, her children may vanish. Sons especially seem to have difficulty witnessing their fathers' infirmities and may respond by staying away. The absence of her children inadvertently deprives their mother of a source of valuable emotional support. Here again is an example of how our culture's rigid gender roles harm both men and women. Men in our society are taught to present strong and invincible personae, only to be viewed in their aging and in illness as weak and disappointing to their offspring.

What Helen De Rosis, M.D., has labeled a "base-line need" in her book, *Women And Anxiety,* is a person toward whom one can feel love or affection directed outward. De Rosis, among others, believes that we can enjoy the feeling of affection or fondness, "without response or participation on the other's part."

She gives as an example a middle-aged person "caring tenderly for difficult, invalid parents": "Expecting nothing in return . . . there is little to impair the warmness of [your] affection . . . and . . . theoretically you could experience outer-directed affection indefinitely, as long as you're not hurt by the other person." If you are hurt, De Rosis goes on to say, "even though you might choose to delude yourself . . . unless you recovered from the hurt, you could not feel as warmhearted as previously."

Now, a question arises here concerning how the caregiver can continue to perform the backbreaking job of caring for her aging invalid relatives, contemporaneously with her other homemaker duties. Is she expected to continue to heal herself from any emotional wounds inflicted by the caregiven angry relatives? Such a woman, exhausted and receiving little support, will likely become bitter, and if in recovery from chemical dependence, she certainly may become vulnerable to relapse.

Claudia, 60, a recovering prescription drug addict and wife of an active alcoholic, was such a woman. She cared for her parents, both in their late eighties, her mother partially paralyzed from a stroke and her father, though ambulatory, forgetful and complaining. They lived with Claudia for three years. Claudia was their sole caregiver, aside from a visiting nurse who appeared twice monthly. Said Claudia:

> I was an absolute wreck, worn out all the time. I didn't even have the energy to go to church on Sunday. I was worried because my own children stopped visiting us, and I felt they didn't like me anymore. I felt lonely and frightened. No one seemed to understand that I just was not able to do it all and keep on smiling. I felt guilty and angry. Then one day after agonizing for months and fretting about what my family and friends would think if I did what I needed to do to take care of myself, I finally made a healthy decision and began to make changes.
>
> With the help of my daughter, I found a sheltered-care situation for my parents nearby that was affordable, but it required that I make a personal monetary sacrifice to do it. Many years ago my parents had given me money in trust for my own later security. I withdrew those savings and placed my parents in a residential nursing home where they could live together. Then I stepped up my 12 Steps. Now I visit my parents without resentment and can really give them the love they deserve. They have made the transition surprisingly well and my father has become involved in chess-playing. I may be poor when I get old, but now at least I have a chance to live to *be* old and I cherish that possibility. Now I can continue to experience my grandchildren growing!
>
> On Thanksgiving night, our entire family visited my parents in the nursing home. My kids, their kids. Everybody. It was a dream come true. Why, my family never did anything like that when my parents lived with me. Everybody was too angry and scared. Not once have I regretted my decision.

Caretaker Characteristics

Caretakers have in common a number of characteristics. While the following is not a definitive list, you may recognize yourself, relatives or friends in some of these descriptions:

• *Caretakers are overextended.* Their schedules are packed from dawn till dark. They take care of their families, walk their dogs, attend to endless domestic chores, report to full-time jobs and stay overtime to finish projects long after everyone else has gone home — the list goes on and on. In this relentless busy-ness, they rarely have a moment to themselves and next to nothing of what they do is for themselves. Most of their efforts are aimed at doing things for others, and they are able to accept little to no assistance. In essence, the caretaker overfunctions. She overdoes the work, but then she also complains about it. And when someone does try to help her, she complains that they are not doing it according to her standards.

• *Caretakers believe that love must be purchased through self-sacrifice and suffering.* This suffering can be accomplished in many ways: by self-degradation, constant self-criticism, loneliness and feeling omitted or rejected and by constantly complaining to others of their burdensome lives. On a metaphysical level a woman's suffering can be manifested through scars on her body, days and nights with migraine headaches and countless physical maladies, especially effective if they can be linked to sacrificial acts performed for others. Without such pain caretakers feel undeserving of love.

• *Caretakers are worried about whether or not they are doing a good job and are often in need of reassurance.* Caretakers are perfectionists, acutely self-conscious and shy, extreme in their concern that they are performing well. Never satisfied with themselves, they try harder and harder. They constantly worry about how they appear to others and are fearful that they will be criticized for being less than perfect. They are devastated by criticism and relentlessly beat themselves up emotionally. They continually seek validation from others.

• *Caretakers are often unwilling or unable to accept compliments or love from other people.* This is truly a paradox: desperately desirous of validation from others, caretakers

have great difficulty accepting it. This is due to their fear
that if they accept compliments, they will lose their own
purpose or role in life, which is to be the one giving
compliments, not receiving them. Caretakers give enormous amounts of energy and concern but can accept little
in return. Caretakers often feel emotionally deprived, resentful and depressed.

• *Caretakers have an extreme need to be needed.* We all need
to be needed, to feel we can make a contribution in the
world. This need, as manifest in the extreme beliefs and
behavior of the caretaker, however, becomes part of a
kind of perverse power play. The caretaker in her convo-
luted perception is essentially saying, "If you fulfill my
extreme need to be needed, I will have power over you."
If you do not need the caretaker, that means you are free,
and therefore you are threatening to her.

• *Caretakers do not know what they need.* Instructed from
the beginning, however subtly, that her whole purpose in
life is to serve her man or the family she would give birth
to, she learned that her needs are always secondary. Her
worst nightmare would be that others deem her selfish or
self-centered, that she cared only about herself. Yet these
may well have been the very criticisms that she did hear
from her family throughout her childhood.

I am continually amazed at the large numbers of women
who firmly believe that their emotional needs are not so
important as those of their spouses or children. In my
therapy practice, one technique I use to determine whether or not someone is a caretaker is to ask her what she
needs emotionally right now. A caretaker does not know,
so out of touch with her needs is she.

• *Caretakers have many acquaintances and few intimate
friends.* Caretakers are surrounded by people to whom
they give, but few of their relationships are close ones.
Intimacy, after all, requires both giving and receiving, a
process called reciprocity, which is an important aspect of
all healthy relationships.

The core issue, difficulty in receiving, extends to other
aspects of older women's lives. This is due in part to their

having lived through the traumas of the Great Depression. For the older woman receiving social services of any kind is often viewed as receiving undeserved charity. Receiving public assistance and disability benefits, for example, is taboo among many proud women. "We can do it ourselves," they will say, or "It will stay in the family; this is nobody else's business," or "I might lean upon my children, but I don't want to take any handouts." Women need to learn that the taxes they have paid earn them access to social services.

The inability to receive radiates to many areas of an older woman's life, from financial aid, to social services, to physical help in getting from the bed to the bathroom. It is of utmost importance in recovery to be able to receive.

• *Caretakers find it difficult to express their anger appropriately.* Often caretakers disperse their anger indirectly in a global and socially acceptable manner, perhaps by becoming tree-huggers, or by working for human rights or animal rights or a charity. This is not to suggest that these are not worthwhile causes, but when a caretaker expresses her anger about homeless kittens but not about her abusive husband, something is very wrong.

• *Caretakers have an extreme need to appear competent and confident.* Desperate to look good, the caretaker makes every effort to demonstrate to herself and to others that she has no problems, that she has everything under control, that in essence she is supermom, superwoman. Approaching life with this posture enables her to appear and sometimes even to feel superior to others. However, she quite likely feels inferior. Older women often vacillate between feelings of superiority and inferiority, between being dominating and controlling and being helpless, needy and clinging. This disparity reflects society's untenable expectation that the young, unprepared bride, despite her lack of healthy role models, miraculously knows how to perform perfectly as a wife and mother, to be a "good woman." Not knowing what she is doing, but terrified because she believes she is supposed to know, the caretaking mother does the next best thing. She *acts* as if she knows what she is doing.

• *Caretakers resist giving up control.* Knowing our limitations is one of the first lifesaving precepts of the 12-Step philosophy. In the attempt to control others or situations outside of themselves caretakers know no limits. Again and again they try to exert control over the world. Miriam exclaimed:

> All my life, I tried to change my alcoholic husband's behavior. And I honestly believed that it was my job as a mother to mold my children's character and behavior. But then, just when I thought I had my children under control, my husband's alcoholism progressed to the point where everything fell apart anyway.

The main job of the caretaker, after all, is to make everything look good: to make ends meet, to be there for her husband and her children and to meet all their needs. Her worth as a wife and mother is externally referenced, based on what she hopes or fears others will think. What a balancing act she has! Frankly, the burden of responsibilities that the caretaker assumes, and the grace with which she often manages to maintain the balance, is incredible. No wonder so many caretakers have bad backs!

• *Caretakers are not heard by their families.* Women are frequently ridiculed by their spouses and their children when they finally speak of their pain. Numerous recovering women have told me that their experience of being listened to and acknowledged in therapy and in their 12-Step meetings was the first positive reinforcement they have received in their entire lives.

The conflicting perspectives of the married couple repeatedly are astonishing. A wife may consider her husband to be emotionally cruel. When confronted, he states she has always been childish and hypersensitive. Those caretaking qualities in the marriage she considers unbearable as she becomes involved in recovery, he continues to consider to be first rate, insisting he is perfectly comfortable with the status quo. Often he becomes angry that she has gone outside the family to broadcast her pain. None of this, he says, is anybody's business but theirs.

Caretakers And Martyrs

Despite its obvious drawbacks, caretaking has its definite benefits, as does any other dysfunctional behavior. If it did not, no one would engage in it. Caretaking is an effective way for many women to have their sick needs met. These women, we joke in my therapy groups, are in Caretaker Heaven. This is a place where women can indulge their overfunctioning and perfectionism and build resentments toward others who are less than perfect. This is a place where women find a pharmaceutical panacea for their body aches and pains, for stress and unhappiness brought on by their behavior, where they have every excuse to indulge in analgesics, antidepressants and tranquilizers.

But Caretaker Heaven eventually makes way for Martyrdom Hell. Caretaking is a progressive disease. Unaddressed, the illness and its sufferer grow worse. A couple of years ago I inadvertently coined a word during a women's therapy group. The word is *martaker,* and it describes a woman with the qualities of a caretaker who is becoming sicker and sicker, heading in the direction of becoming a martyr.

The caretaker is the fetus of the martyr; caretaking is the learning period for martyrdom. Caretakers accept abuse and are involved in not hurting others, regardless of the cost to themselves. The caretaker tries to hide her feelings about her life. She acts as if she doesn't have anger or bitterness. She utters such statements as, "Well, it's not as bad as it could be" or "I'll try twice as hard next time." Unable and unwilling to protect herself emotionally and physically, the caretaker is an easy target for frequent abuse. Over time, she becomes a victim in every sense of the word. At a certain point she has no choice left but to become a martyr.

The martyr is openly bitter, resentful, confused, isolated, critical, perfectionistic and pessimistic. Martyrs feel
disconnected from themselves and from others, and they
wallow in self-pity. The caretaker-turned-martyr will
make such statements as, "After all I've done!" or "What
did I do to deserve this?" To their children they say, "You'll
be the death of me yet!" or "How could you do this to
me?" One caretaker-turned-martyr I know bought a
gravestone and had the bill sent to her daughter, whom
she considered to be an ingrate.

Sometimes martyrs pout and withdraw angrily. They
exist in an aura of disappointment and disillusionment.
They keep close track of others' "sins of omission" —
birthday cards unsent, phone calls not made. At the same
time deep down they believe that they themselves are bad
people. They suffer an overwhelming sense of shame and
inadequacy. Martyrs dwell in a state that combines blaming others, self-flagellation and self-pity.

"Caretakers are predictable, steady, useful and safe,"
said Thomas Wright of the Johnson Institute. "They are
sensitive to the needs of others and are also boring.
They are not particularly enjoyable. They rarely smile
and laugh."

The caretaker becomes boring because she expends all
her energy focusing on other people rather than growing
and developing as a person herself. She rarely smiles and
laughs because the life she chooses to lead leaves her
exhausted, disappointed and bitter.

The sooner the caretaker gives up this behavior, the
better. The caretaking wife and mother must shed the
grandiosity that she has indulged in over the years, the
illusion that she can both save and control everybody. For
years she has been playing the role of the royal matriarch,
sometimes covertly. She must stop taking care of other
people and start giving care to herself. The time has come
to abdicate the throne.

Claire

Claire *was* a caretaker *extraordinaire*. Fear was the issue at her very core; it was her greatest motivator and her greatest monster. It lived in her for 60 years.

Claire is 62, divorced, urban, born in poverty of illiterate immigrant Russian Jews. Kiev was all her parents knew, she says. After their immigration to Chicago during the Great Depression, their fear of starvation kept them bound to their native culture and language. The youngest of three children, Claire as a toddler was handed the role of her mother's caretaker, and at the age of five began to learn the go-between role, sent by her mother, who had several chronic illnesses, to obtain money from her father on payday to be able to pay the rent before he either gambled it away or misspent it. On those occasions when her father refused to give her rent money, Claire felt like a failure for not providing for her mother. The family, unable to pay rent regularly, moved often, leaving Claire feeling fearful, inadequate and rootless. Her mother's message to Claire: "You are the only one keeping me from death. You are my only reason to live."

When she was 15, Claire quit school to care for her ailing mother. She also became the chief caregiver to an infant nephew who was left in the home of her parents, and she began working as a salesperson in a department store. With her first paycheck, she took her mother to dinner in a "nice restaurant."

Claire married at 18. She had two daughters, born 18 months apart. Claire was their sole caregiver. "My husband often complained that children were an aggravation. After I married, as long as my mother was alive, I was the prize that my mother and my husband struggled to win." The ongoing competition between Claire's spouse and her mother was, more accurately, a battle for Claire's time and energy. Their clamoring was constant and clearly a manifestation of their own untreated child-adult issues that they painfully loaded onto Claire as "caring."

For Claire, meeting their every need was her only way to feel adequate. "I never could quite feel adequate, though," says Claire, now in recovery and feeling better with each new day, "because I could never quite do it well enough for them." Striving to feel adequate for Claire could mean getting up in the middle of the night to prepare a meal for her impulsive and demanding husband or taking a bus across town in subzero weather to accompany her mother to the doctor's office, which was located less than a block from her mother's home.

Claire has been in recovery from co-dependence for three years. She studied for and earned her GED; currently she studies art at a major university in the Midwest.

> What is really important is that I now realize I do not need the unconditional approval from my daughters to be okay with myself. I know now they will not stop loving me and I am no longer devastated by their criticism. I understand why young women of today don't want to be like their mothers. It is astonishing when I hear my grown daughters saying the same things to me that I heard my mother say to me and which I said to my daughters when they were children, such as, "I know that is a favorite dress of yours, dear, but you have others which would flatter you more." Now I tell them what I wear is just fine for me. And only last week, one of my daughters told me not to make funny sounds when I eat. I was happy I could simply smile and tell her I hoped getting used to gum surgery would be different for her if that ever became necessary. It's too late to parent them, but I can still role model. And I'm learning it's never too late to draw boundaries! And guess what? I just don't feel that fear today.

CHAPTER THREE

The Recovering Older Woman

The recovering older woman is comfortable with herself as she ages, accepting of herself. Doubts and fears regarding loss of sexual attractiveness according to society's standards no longer plague her. Her sense of self-worth precludes her victimization by grey hairs and wrinkles.

The recovering older woman demonstrates authenticity in who she is and how she behaves. She is centered, living from the very nucleus of herself, where she finally finds the self-appreciation and nurture that she has for so many years yearned to have.

The recovering older woman is aware of her needs and acts on them. She sets daily goals, keeps her body clean and healthy and her spirits high. Her most intimate and satisfying relationship is with herself.

However, she enjoys close relationships with friends, children and partners. In her partnerships she attends to her own needs first. If she has grown children, she interacts with them as friends and enjoys them as adults rather than as children. She shows gentle concern and abstains from caretaking. She knows when and to whom to say yes or no. She knows her limitations, both physical and emotional.

The recovering older woman exercises personal freedom, daring to do what she had not previously consciously considered possible or acceptable. She takes new and considered risks, both emotional and social. She pursues with enthusiasm, perhaps even passion, interests outside her home. She need not be a leader in her community, but she *may* become one. Whatever role she chooses is the one she is ready for.

The recovering older woman is not fearful of looking at her past, albeit examining her own pain and changing the patterns of behavior that caused others pain have been most difficult. She exchanges blame and disappointment in her past for discovery in the present.

The recovering older woman looks like any other woman on the street, but when a sister in recovery meets her, something unique happens. Older women in recovery recognize each other. They see in each other a woman like themselves, a woman who is learning not to yell at her family, who has ceased gossiping about her neighbors and friends and who is learning to make choices for herself. A woman, for example, who may choose not to serve her husband when he says, "Bring me a cup of coffee." A woman who may instead say, "Well, the coffee's right up there on the kitchen shelf, and you can make some, just one tablespoon per cup, fill the pot and let it boil — and while you're there, could you bring me a cup, please, and maybe put a little cinnamon in it because I'd like to have a cup with you."

On the following page are brief glimpses into the lives of three healthy recovering older women:

Lillian

We were walking together after an AA meeting on Chicago's Southside, this dear woman, now 73, whom I have known all my sober life. I asked her how she views her own aging in recovery.

"It ain't over 'til it's over! I'm still working!" And she threw back her fine black head, fairly cackling to the skies, her words of joy flung out ahead of us. Lillian has a face that reminds me of those bouncing smiling faces you see pasted on children's toys. Just looking at her makes me feel good. "If you're gonna write about *my* life, you'd better make space, honey. Lord knows there's a long time to write about!" And then she began to share her secrets.

Hers is not an unusual story, unless you haven't heard about the common plight of many black women born early in the twentieth century in the South, in Alabama, Arkansas, Louisiana, where little girls were raped routinely on the farms and plantations and where babies were sex objects before they were barely dry from the womb. Where alcohol was as common as cotton.

Lillian journeyed with her three children to Chicago in the mid 1950s. "I had an old Dodge with no spare tire and fifteen dollars in my pocket. When I got to the city, I dumped my kids at my aunt's house and went out on the street to get drunk. I stayed drunk for eight years — until it just didn't work anymore. The guilt got stronger than the booze. I got sober in 1963. There wasn't a place to get detoxed then, so I just shook for about a year and prayed a lot. But the Lord helped me. Then I went into a training program and learned bookkeeping. I've been sober and working ever since!" What was the most important factor in Lillian's continuing recovery, I asked. She paused and reflected carefully for a few moments. "The Lord," she sighed, not smiling now, "The Lord."

Lenore

We sat drinking tea by candlelight in my motor home after I had arrived after dark at the reservation, as we had arranged. Lenore is anonymous and wants to keep it that way. She did not want her neighbors seeing me scrambling around her house with my "Clean and Sober" sticker above the license plate. She doesn't even allow me to use the name of her Native American tribe. "Just say I'm a redskin," she giggled. "Most people are ashamed they drink," she continued, "but I'm afraid to tell people I don't drink. My neighbors all think I'm just on the wagon for a while because I had some stomach surgery. But I'm really a recovering alcoholic, too." For Lenore, 57, it was a cultural command to attend her alcoholic husband as his companion at social functions. This went on for 20 years, with Lenore drinking every day with her husband. "I was very sick. I wanted to stop, but I couldn't," she said, "I am a teacher. I speak and teach my native language to my people, and the alcohol always kept me from teaching. I was not reliable." But for Lenore to stop drinking was to alienate her from her friends. Only after her husband died did she find sobriety, and secretly. "Now I teach my language," she said proudly, "and I am free. I have not had one slip for three years. I am helping my people again." She spoke gently, "I am very happy."

Maria

Maria is Chicano, a recovering alcoholic in AA for five years with four children still living at home. She grew up in California's San Joaquin Valley. Her practicing alcoholic husband left a year ago, with no word of his whereabouts or financial assistance from him since. She says she grew up in the American dream, but in a very distinct shade of brown. She talks slowly, not slowly as though she has to consider each word or as if concerned about stuttering, but slowly as she moves in her own rhythm, from her own sense of timing.

She has a lean face, greying hair. She laughs frequently, laughs at the ironies and contradictions of her recovery. She is 57 and her brown eyes close slightly when she laughs, her broad face filled with feeling. She throws her head back, her eyes are crinkly behind her glasses and the sound is immediate and full, you know she is not laughing at you. Moments later, when she makes her point, her eyes are wide and clear and deep. One knows nothing will stop Maria for very long. She uses her hands to talk, to smooth the air, to ask questions. When she responds to questions, she takes her time considering, looking, staring into the air or straight into you.

"Sober does not mean you do not play," she says. "My children and my grandchildren, they go to ACoA meetings in the town nearby. We are not ashamed of our disease anymore. They ride their bikes, and sometimes they get rides with one of their teachers. They play and roll around with me after I get home from work. We are beautiful and healthy. And we try to keep clean in every sense of the word. This keeps me happy with life." She is a woman who loves silence as well and listens to the songs of birds. A woman of the earth, a woman of labor . . . a woman of spirit.

Recovery Defined

People often ask me, in my dual roles as therapist and recovering woman, what recovery is. Most simply, recovery means learning to live in the present moment aware and accepting of our feelings and getting our needs met without inflicting pain on ourselves or others. A person may be in recovery from any of the multitude of dysfunctions addressed in 12-Step programs, among them alcoholism, addiction to prescription or narcotic drugs or other chemicals, and co-dependence. The primary focus of this book is on our recovery from co-dependence, that skeleton of societal imbalance around which generations of dysfunctioning families have twisted themselves.

Recovery From Societal Oppression

I view recovery from yet another perspective: as a woman sensitive to women's issues. Recovery from co-dependence is largely recovery from societal oppression. It would be all but impossible to describe recovery for older women without referring to the tenets of feminism as they have been formulated over a century of struggle. Significant among the fundamentals of feminism are recovering from the attitude of helpless passivity handed to us by our families of origin and society as a whole; learning to be self-reliant and assertive; and releasing the sex-role restrictions imposed upon women, men and children, thus directing ourselves toward a higher degree of equality among us all.

My work and my life's purpose are essentially based on my feminist political beliefs. This is why I was drawn to the co-dependent recovery movement in the first place. To get what we want, to get our needs met without hurting someone or ourselves — this is feminism and this is healing from co-dependence. It is not a matter of having power over anybody else. It is not a matter of burning bras or having someone hold the door open for us. It is about being free to be as good as we can be, as we want to be, to do our personal best — whether we are female or male.

Aiming toward equanimity is a departure from the hierarchal nature of dysfunctional systems. Aiming toward freedom from the restrictive socially prescribed roles that make prisoners of both sexes flies in the face of co-dependence. Are women really lacking in the ability to take care of themselves, to solve analytic problems or to lift heavy boxes? Are women meant to endure sexual harassment on the street and in the workplace? Are men really insensitive, unfeeling creatures, innately incapable of tending house or being actively engaged in raising their children? Or of weeping? Of course not.

Yet these are the sex-linked stereotypes passed on from one generation to the next, even today in these seemingly more liberated times. In the process of cutting through these falsehoods in our recovery from co-dependence, we make positive changes, not only in our current living situations, but also as mothers and grandmothers of the next generation ultimately laying the groundwork for a healthier world.

Special Challenges To Older Women In Recovery

The older woman's traditional role in our culture contains a number of characteristics that make her decision to recover and the process of recovery itself difficult. None of these is insurmountable. But being forewarned is, after all, being forearmed.

• It is an unfortunate fact that recovery from co-dependence by older women is frequently viewed as aberrant or even as deviant behavior. In going against the grain of society's very carefully hewn lumber, our assigned roles as older women, we risk getting splinters. It has been written that war ruins armies. Recovery ruins those nuclear families that are in dysfunction, enmeshed in the wrath of generations of untenable yet frozen commands of authority. Married couples find themselves stuck in the social order of a century ago, when rule-of-thumb was law (a husband could beat his wife and children if he used a stick no wider than his thumb). Little wonder, then, that the national divorce rate continues to escalate.

• Older women are faced with recovering from not only one dysfunctional role but from two: that of the abused, neglected or battered child from her dysfunctional family of origin, and that of the mother of her own dysfunctional family. She suffers twofold pain — twofold anger, twofold losses and so on — as she sorts through the past to create a healthier present.

• Feelings of guilt and experiences of rejection by those she loves may ensue when the recovering older woman finally begins to stand up for herself, which may mean, for example, choosing not to provide child care for grandchildren while her children are employed outside the home or demanding that she have an equal voice with her husband in all of their financial affairs.

• The older woman faces hardships that accompany the unavoidable realities of physical aging and mortality.

She may be recently widowed or retired and undergoing stressful adaptation to these dramatic changes. She may be suffering from physical illness or dealing with illness in her spouse or others close to her. The natural and sometimes dramatic decline of her physical self can accelerate her sense of powerlessness, even to a traumatic level.

• The older woman may have reduced mobility. She may find herself dependent upon her children, the very people who may resent her for what they consider years of bad parenting. Her grown children and other people, out of apparent concern for her, may prevent her from driving her car or otherwise getting out in the world. Women in such situations tend to become isolated, especially in rural areas. Unable to reach the assistance they need, their potential for recovery is greatly reduced.

• Recovery involves learning new skills for interaction in the world. Our society challenges the older woman to develop an additional layer of new skills with which to cope with ageism, ranging from the neglect behavior by public employees to, unfortunately, the condescending attitudes of many counselors and therapists. Older women in recovery often have to make a special effort to learn new ways to assert themselves in getting what they need. Neither silence nor loud demands get the job done.

• Older recovering women may have a greater struggle with certain emotional and psychological aspects of the recovery process. The older woman, traditionally the giver of nurture, tends to be resistant to receiving nurture from others. Learning to give and to receive love is essential to the healing process. Furthermore, well-rehearsed in a social role in which she is to be simultaneously inferior and superior, the older woman may have a hard time establishing a healthy middle ground between the passive "I-don't-know-anything" sycophant and the overbearing matriarch who has been socialized to pretend she has nothing to learn from anyone.

• Finally, the older woman may have difficulty being honest and direct with others. "People-pleasers" who are fearful of hurting others' feelings and terrified of being rejected themselves, they feel tortured at the prospect of needing to confront family, friends or even peers in a therapy group. Yet this very honesty and forthrightness is precisely what is required to move herself toward a life free of the pain of co-dependence.

Advantages To Older Women

Older women also enjoy some advantages in recovery by virtue of their age. Major among them is that older women have lived a vast number of years and have amassed many more life experiences from which to draw as compared to younger women. This wisdom comes to their service in recovery. Another advantage is that in some corners of our universe, being older *does* command respect. When people are willing to view older women not as authority figures but as people who can share wisdom, then a more mutually beneficial relationship ensues. A number of my clients, in fact, come to me specifically seeking an older woman as a therapist.

Everything of worth requires some effort, it is often said, some struggle. If this is true, recovery is worth every effort, its rewards plentiful. Recovery is not just a matter of feeling happier, having better relationships or enjoying a renewed sense of meaning and purpose in life, although these certainly are among the benefits. But in some cases, recovery from co-dependence can even be a matter of life or death.

The 80-year-old mother of one of my clients has been at home taking care of her husband, who suffers from dementia. The mother finally took him to a day-care center, but for just one day. Although the man is not in full possession of his mental faculties, his co-dependent wife insists upon leaving to him the decision about whether or not he will go back to the center. She is afraid that if she makes the decision, he will be angry and blame her. Should he choose not to return to the center, this 80-year-old woman, herself in need of help, will be left with sole responsibility for his physical and emotional needs. This pathetic and frightening situation, not unusual in our society today, illustrates all too clearly how crucial recovery from co-dependence can be. Many of my clients have said, "This is a matter of living or dying. This situation is killing me, however softly."

Denial Versus Willingness

Perhaps more than anything else people in recovery possess one crucial quality: the willingness to become aware. My clients, my sisters in AA and other 12-Step programs and the recovering women I have interviewed all demonstrate the willingness to look honestly at themselves and their lives and to face the possibility that they have been going about things in the wrong way, in a sick way, as a means of survival in a sick family or social system.

Coming to such an awareness is anything but easy. The disease of co-dependence has many parts stretching across vast territories of our being. It is physiological, psychological, cultural-sociological, volitional, emotional and spiritual. The core of the psychological aspect of the disease is *denial*. It is a disease that does not want us to know we have a disease. Denial is further fed by our culture, which keeps family dysfunction a secret.

Emotional pain does not lend itself easily to quantitative analysis. Sometimes a group therapy client asks me apologetically, "But do I really belong here? My pain is not half as bad as the others." Obviously she does belong there, but denial and numbing have blocked her pain. All human beings have a right to their own pain. But seeing others express their pain can seem overwhelming to someone who does not yet feel her own.

"Why not just let bygones be bygones?" some women ask. But for many of us the past cannot be dispensed with so easily. If nostalgia brings you more pain than sweetness of memory, then that is lasting pain, and there is work to be done. If singing or hearing songs brings on the blues that linger for days, or if you begin to obsess on a person or an event of long ago, then there is work to be done. If you are reading a poem, story or diary that hearkens to a time of excessive pain, if tears begin to flow and seem unstoppable or if you feel overpowering bitterness or anger, then there's work to be done.

Anything that interrupts our balance, centeredness and groundedness for a period of time is a clue that we have issues to address. Finding ourselves self-diagnosing our physical illnesses — feeling a pain in my foot and then telling myself I must have bone cancer — or reaching out excessively to doctors, calling them every day for reassurance, are signs that we have unfinished emotional business. Older co-dependent women experienced the same difficulties in their childhoods that their own children struggle with in recovery today, but admitting this is often more difficult in older women, their layers of denial thicker and more impenetrable. For the woman who was paralyzed in the pain of her childhood, who grew up maintaining "secrets" and "shoulds" as her codes for living, denial has become a long-standing way of life.

Most women believe that in their roles as wives and mothers they have done the best that they could, but I'm not sure that we have. Most older women view as normal the oppression that they suffered, and thus inculcated in their own children those patterns of emotional deprivation that they experienced in their own childhoods. When I ask older women what they must give up in order to get to the reality of their childhood, frequently they weep and say that they would have to give up their fantasy that the way they had lived was "right" and "good," that their parents were loving and healthy. Of the 110 women I interviewed, more than 80 found it difficult to acknowledge that their own mothers' values were skewed. Said Jenny:

> I was absolutely desolate for weeks after I identified my mother's verbal violence as bad parenting and emotional abuse. Before that, the abuse had passed merely as strict disciplining. That is what I passed on to my children . . . and now I see my children doing it to my grandchildren.

To admit dysfunction requires humility, and the older woman customarily has not chosen this path. More familiar to her is the self-martyring road, even in her recovery. How often do we hear women say in AA meetings, "I worked so long and so hard, and now my children just hate me. There is no gratitude! It's so unfair, after all I've done. They say I've done it all wrong. And it's too late to do it over." In direct proportion to the amount of sacrifice she made for her children, the unrecovering co-dependent older woman expects her reward. Cynical and disappointed in life, she pouts, withdraws in silence and resists change at all costs.

Denial finally falls by the wayside when we are able to experience a state of what we shall name *personal co-dependence*. One of my professors in graduate school and my mentor, the late Dr. William Gideon, introduced me to his concept of *personal alcoholism*, that very deep, profound acknowledgment, far beyond just mouthing the words or going to AA meetings, that on every level of our being we really own the disease, alcoholism. To do this meant to me that if I wanted to live, I had no more choice to drink alcohol again in this lifetime than I had to bring my parents back from the dead.

In this manner I became less bothered by the voice of denial, the voice that, even today, sings to me once a year or so, in the middle of an unusually stressful workday, "Oh, Helen, you haven't had a drink for nearly 22 years . . . maybe you can have just one after work . . . and maybe you really aren't alcoholic, after all . . ." It is then that I consciously pull from my memory bank one of a multitude of ghastly recollections from my drinking days, to remind me that my power over alcohol is my abstinence from it. And then, remembering that I have a chronic and fatal disease, as quickly as I can, I get myself to an AA meeting, where I find warmth and safety and acceptance. That is how *personal alcoholism* works for me.

In the same way we must develop that sense awareness of our own co-dependence that is so profound that we are conscious of it on all levels . . . *personal co-dependence*.

Ultimately to admit to co-dependence is not a confession of being *bad*, but an admission of *illness*. Recovery is not the process of reforming in order to overcome bad behavior, but of healing from illness. Until the co-dependent woman finally comes to this way of thinking, she will forever flounder in the argument of right and wrong, good or bad, and she will remain powerless to change. If she has done wrong, it is because of her illness, not because she is inherently bad. Admitting an illness means that she can heal. Finally she can take responsibility for having made those errors, make amends for them and change herself through changing her behaviors.

An End To Postponement

We all hear people making excuses for not quitting their addictions: "Well, I'll quit smoking after Christmas" or "I'll stop taking my antidepressants as soon as my husband goes on the road or when the kids get out of the house." This is postponement, and we must not postpone recovery from addiction, whether that addiction is to alcohol, chemicals or people in our families. For the older woman timing is especially important. Procrastination is a very big part of the disease from which we are attempting to recover. It is important that we not wait one day longer. There is no easy time to do it. Addictions are progressive diseases that, when left unchecked, never get any better. They are fatal.

We must not view as a sacrifice the process of "giving up" those things that are destroying us. We *quit* our addictions. We do not give them up. To say we quit drinking alcohol, we quit taking Valium, we quit overeating, we quit controlling our families, is simply to say we quit practicing those behaviors that were killing us. In this slow and life-long recovery process, this journey spiraling upward, we simply quit all of our addictions.

Many a woman says her daily mottos and reads her daily meditations in her recovery from chemical dependence, with one hand behind her back, "white-knuckling" it — she may go to five AA meetings a week and still contemplate suicide, still wish her husband would drop dead. In the recovery from co-dependence as well as chemical dependence, she can open both hands in front of herself freely, with self-love and without unexpressed rage, guilt and shame.

For myself, I needed time to rid my body of the residuals of alcohol and other drugs, including nicotine and marijuana. I needed time to develop a healthy approach to food, learning to eat nutritionally that resulted in my losing 125 excess pounds. I needed time to clear away waves of shame from my years of active alcoholism and to deal with the profound sense of grief I felt at the loss of alcohol. After all, before it became my betrayer, alcohol had been my closest ally, protecting me from my deepest pain. Most of all, I needed time to get to know myself.

Many of my clients required a period of several years to stop using all their drugs, ranging from heroin to caffeine. It is often in the aftermath of this cleansing crisis, after undergoing tremendous changes in the physical, psychological, social, emotional and spiritual areas of their lives, that the time for recovery from co-dependence begins. It is at this point that most of my co-dependent clients today engage me for therapy. "I know something's wrong," they will say. "I know I'm unhappy, that I'm not doing it right, that I'm not getting what I want — but I don't know what it is." This is the essence of co-dependence. And this is the other half of the healing that began with abstinence from alcohol or chemicals. For me this was a new phase of reconstruction, the beginning of emotional stability, as well as the heightening of personal and spiritual awareness.

Some older women approaching this juncture feel it is too late for them. They feel left out. They feel the need to be in control but have largely lost control of their lives. They have a sense of not being understood by their children. They feel disappointed. They have worked very hard and sacrificed much of their adult life for their children and now are not being rewarded. This has been

called the *empty-nest syndrome*, but the problem extends
beyond the children having grown up and moved out.
These women suffer from a deep sense of emptiness and
lack of fulfillment. Most of them feel inferior. And under-
lying all of this is a sense of uselessness and worthlessness
in the world. They feel resigned, lonely, undesirable and
unattractive. In recovery these women afford themselves
a whole new world of discovery in which they feel embraced, challenged and inspired.

The Process Of Recovery

Most people are looking for a how-to manual, a quick
fix, an easy way to stop the pain, to fill up the big black
hole inside, to diminish the cloud that seems to hang over
their heads, to make right instantly what seems to be
wrong, to make healthy what appears to be unhealthy.
But the flow of recovery is dependent upon the unique
needs and pace of the individual.

Change comes slowly, baby-step by baby-step. As co-
dependence authority Mary Lee Zawadski describes it,
we must take the whole of this mountainous process and
"chunk it down" into manageable parts. This way we can
finally begin to get a handle on a life that, as is stated in
the 12 Steps, has become unmanageable.

Every week in my therapy groups we each talk about
one small behavior that we can change in the coming
week that can make a difference in our lives, that can be
sustained toward a healthier lifestyle or workstyle or re-
lationship-style. This is how people change, one small step
at a time, week after week. But the weeks and months and
years add up, and the accumulated changes can be profound. We trust ourselves, and we commit to going
through whatever it takes to bring us happiness, trusting
that on the other side of that mountain there is something
better than we have known.

So there is no magic trick. If you are suffering from
addiction or co-dependence, if you have pain and guilt and
people are telling you that you did things the wrong way

and you know that you want to vindicate yourself, there are indeed ways you can heal and feel better about yourself and others.

Attend 12-Step Meetings

Depending on your situation, your mobility and availability of a meeting, get yourself to a 12-Step meeting. If your husband is drinking, go to an Al-Anon meeting. If you yourself are drinking to excess, go to an AA meeting. What is "excess"? Because of my denial system, I did not believe I was an alcoholic, but I stopped drinking and went to AA anyway. Six months passed before I realized I had been a falling-down drunk. In the meantime I saw that the people in AA meetings were good to me, giving attention to me to an extent that no one had in my life. So I kept going to meetings, and I started getting well.

If you are ready to deal with co-dependence, go to a CODA (Co-dependents Anonymous) meeting. Or try ACoAs (Adult Children of Alcoholics). If you are new to 12-Step meetings, you should know that you can just go and listen. You don't have to talk. And if you don't like that meeting, try another. Newcomers to the program are always advised to try at least five meetings. Chances are you will quickly find one where you will feel comfortable.

Many older women told me, incidentally, that for years they believed they had no need for Al-Anon, ACoAs or CODA because their fathers or mothers who were alcoholic were long dead or they were divorced or widowed from their alcoholic husbands. The fact of the matter is, the influence these people had upon you perseveres, and hence these 12-Step groups are still appropriate for you.

If you are unable to find a 12-Step meeting in your area, you can form one. It only takes three people to have a 12-Step meeting. Locate a counselor to help you get started, perhaps through a local university, hospital or senior service agency. Such people are available and willing to visit you. You may be able to find lectures on recovery-related topics. Many women belong to Bible-study groups, book-review groups, symphony-listening groups or morning-walking groups. Just getting yourself to a place where you can exchange ideas with others and talk about your pain in a structured setting is sometimes all it takes to get started. If you are in an abusive situation, get out of it. Call a social service agency *now*. Don't wait.

It is essential to use your creativity to get what you need to be sober and clean and sane. Many women I interviewed by phone told me that they are in nursing homes and cannot get to 12-Step meetings. So why not start a meeting in a nursing home? Meetings come in all sizes and shapes. One group of women in Colorado calls itself the Jump for Joy Women. All of them, 80 years old and older, meet once a week for an AA meeting and then follow it with physical exercises. Near Minneapolis, there is a telephone AA group of people who are confined to wheelchairs. There's a dating group of people over 60 in San Diego who are recovering in AA. There are even several 12-Step groups that tour different parts of the world together. That is how I visited Europe for the first time, nearly fifteen years ago.

Find A Therapist

I have always loved the sound of women's voices in a group. Even after all these years as a therapist, I sometimes stand for a moment's pause in the tiny kitchen of my condominium in Chicago where I work and listen to the soft rumbling laughter of women as they assemble for a group. The sounds of women's voices are sacred to me, soft and safe, musical and comforting. And little wonder. They are, after all, the sounds that family nurturers make. In therapy groups, women nurture themselves and one another.

In seeking a therapist as a healing co-dependent you must find one who follows the 12 Steps or works with co-dependency issues. Not all therapists do. In the same way that certain types of medical treatment require a specialist, therapeutic treatment for dependency issues requires a specialist. Many people have related unfortunate stories about being in therapy for months or even years with little benefit, years during which the therapist never addressed the client's problem with drinking or prescription drugs, smoking or overeating. Worse yet, some therapists view co-dependent behavior the same way that society as a whole does — as a woman's normal role.

To locate an appropriate therapist, ask women whom you trust in 12-Step meetings if they know someone to recommend. Then interview your potential therapist in an initial appointment to consider whether you will work well together. You may feel, by the way, that you would rather see a female than a male therapist, but a man may be equally qualified and empathic in helping you work through your issues. The choice is yours. If you do not have the financial resources for private therapy, a hospital, a university or a government agency may have professionals on staff at a cost you can afford.

The Therapeutic Process In Brief

Recovery is reaching deep down into the places in our psyche where the disease of co-dependence has its roots. We begin to inspect and evaluate the values, beliefs and behaviors of our past and recognize a present need to change them. The process, as I stated earlier, is always an individual one. The strength in a person's recovery is her ability to retain those concepts that are healthful and to eschew those that are victimizing her. We cannot trifle with the trust and self-knowledge of the older recovering woman to know what issues she needs to address, and when.

I see clients both individually and in groups. I encourage the latter, based on the notion demonstrated again and again that the dysfunctional behaviors that plague us in the outside world will emerge within the group. What happens in the therapy group is a microcosm of what happens in the world. More specifically, emerging in the group as working material are many of the survival techniques that group members learned in the past, behaviors that served them well in dysfunctional families, but that today prove to be unhealthy. These behaviors block the way to intimacy in relationships, interfering with communicating with friends and associates and partners, children and other family members.

In therapy groups, we learn to speak to people about our feelings directly and honestly. We learn to communicate exactly what we feel rather than in broad generalities. Instead of saying we feel bad or good, we open ourselves to sharing more definitively our expressions of feeling ashamed or angry or proud or joyful. We strive to stay aware of our thoughts and our feelings and to live with them. We learn the ways we have spent years suppressing or avoiding them. We learn that we are in charge of changing them. And as such we proceed toward the healthy goal of living in one dimension, in the *here and now*. Throughout the group process we help each other. Observing each other, we become aware of the dysfunctional roles that we have played in our families of origin and that we may continue to play. We learn to read each other's body messages. We risk to confront and challenge each other. We support and encourage each other. And slowly and surely we feel healthier.

"How long will this take?" a client will frequently ask during her first session. The answer depends on four main factors. First, her willingness to examine thoroughly the roles she was assigned in her dysfunctional family. Second, her honesty in ascertaining how much mileage she gets from continuing to play those roles today. Third, she must become willing to relinquish those roles. And fourth is the rapidity with which she is able to learn new behaviors.

No two women are the same, nor are any two recovery processes. Just as the constantly changing moon determines the tides and as we women have physical cycles in our lives, each of us is unique in our struggles toward recovery and serenity. We determine what our issues are; we choose our own changing according to the timing of our personal healing cycle.

For many older women, the greatest difficulty in co-
dependent recovery is that first step: to leave the familiar
and oppressive situation that has more than a half-century
of familiarity clinging to it. Indeed, some already know a
great deal about what they are feeling and what they
want. They make vast emotional leaps and healthy
changes only after they make that initial and most difficult
change of taking leave of a killing environment. One met-
aphor women frequently use is the yanking up of deeply
entrenched roots.

Felicia

I am speaking with Felicia, 60, recovering from what
she has described as "passive caretaking." A secretary, she
has been forced into early retirement due to a heart condition that she attributes to 40 years of stressful living.
Self-analytic and verbally explicit, she has had no formal
counseling or therapy prior to our initial session on this
day. She has attended Al-Anon and ACoA meetings for
one year and complains that, although she believes she
needs ACoA meetings, she feels she does not belong in a
meeting where others are half her chronological age.

She comes to therapy fresh from a divorce court,
where she has just ended a battering, childless, alcohol-
plagued 30-year marriage to an unrecovering adult child
of two alcoholics. She has named overspending as her
addiction. Her face is drawn and tired. She appears de-
pleted of energy, and her voice trembles with fear as she
pours out her plight of powerlessness. The following is a
direct quote, in part, offered on tape by Felicia during
our first session:

> I just don't feel adequate anywhere. I am afraid I cannot
> live without a man, and I do not know how to have healthy
> interaction with anyone. I am shocked to learn that I don't
> know how to make unilateral decisions. My own father
> was severe and oppressive in my family of origin. He often
> told me I had no grit. Then my husband made all the
> arrangements when I was married, from choosing our pets

to the kind of food we ate. He picked out the clothes I wore. I feel ashamed to tell you that, because I am afraid you'll see me as weak and pitiful and stupid. Every choice I make now leaves me doubtful and anxious. I am also bored. And now, when I tell you that, I feel ashamed. I cannot do anything gracefully. Although I have had some relief since the divorce and know that I had to do it to live, I feel more rejected now than I did all the years I was suffering from physical violence. Somehow, I must have felt reassured as long as I was being beaten! [Pause] That's how I knew my father loved me, I guess.

As she speaks Felicia does not realize that already she has made a gigantic beginning in her recovery. Leaving an abusive marriage, getting the divorce, attending 12-Step meetings, cutting up her charge cards, were the first actions that have paved the way for safe thinking and feeling. Now she can grieve her losses, reclaim her lost spirit and make the behavior alterations essential to the attitudinal changes that she will need to develop a healthy self-concept. She was not able to see that for herself, however, until we began to set up her Recovery Spiral/ Glitch Graph.

The Recovery Spiral/Glitch Graph

Throughout our recovery process we consistently move upward in the Recovery Spiral (see Figure 3.1).

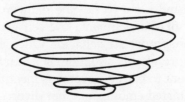

Figure 3.1   Recovery Spiral

Occasionally though, and perhaps more frequently in the beginning of recovery, we encounter glitches, slight relapses. The Glitch Graph (see Figure 3.2) is a cross section of the Recovery Spiral. These mini-relapses, although not essential or even desirable in chemical addiction recovery, are necessary in co-dependent recovery. In these glitches we come face to face with the very behaviors that we need to change. We discover the behaviors that are creating pain in our lives, and we learn how to change, to grow.

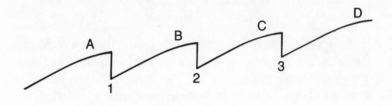

Figure 3.2   Glitch Graph

Figure 3.2 is the Glitch Graph for Felicia. Prior to the start of **Ascending Line A,** Felicia was at her bottom. She was totally in her disease: She had issues around low self-esteem, lack of control, trust, all-or-nothing thinking, fear of abandonment and a high tolerance for inappropriate behavior. Her husband battered her and controlled even her most basic needs.

During **Ascending Line A,** she started to go to ACoA and Al-Anon meetings, left her husband and retained a divorce lawyer. **Glitch 1** happened when she moved back in with her husband for a week. She had come face to face with her fear of abandonment, low self-esteem and high tolerance for inappropriate behavior. Once she realized the untenable nature of this situation, she started **Ascending Line B.** She went to battered women's meetings, cut up her credit cards, started emoting and her divorce became final. At the height of **Ascending Line B,** she was hit with depression because of her feeling that she was unemployable.

At this point she sought out my service as a therapist. In the process of helping herself to see how far she had come, she hit **Glitch 2.** She took over the planning of her niece's wedding. Her disease kicked in with control and compulsive/obsessive behavior. She returned to her familiar family role as broadcaster/news carrier. During **Ascending Line C,** Felicia continued going to ACoA and Al-Anon meetings; she was abstinent, was successful in school and expanded her support network. At **Glitch 3,** Felicia broke her elbow and called her husband for support, which he did not give her. Again, she was deep in her low self-esteem and fear of abandonment.

One important point to remember: No matter how many glitches we experience, or how deep they may seem to us to be, we never go back to the beginning. We are always moving upward on the spiral.

Change At Any Age

In the late 1970s I attended many lectures by a woman who made a great impression on me, Dr. Barbara Brown, the mother of biofeedback. One of her concepts in particular strongly affected my consciousness: As long as life exists in a cell, and we are capable of thought and understanding, we can change our behavior. Doing so may be difficult, but we *can* change, as long as there is life.

Truly, change is possible at any age. The common description of someone being "old and set in her ways" is really a description of someone who does not want to change, rather than someone who is incapable of change. I am reminded of a woodcarver I met in Arizona, a man who whittled away at hard pieces of wood, caressing each block of wood, patiently turning them into whistles. He told me that he really likes to get to the wood's inside, where it is softer and more malleable and he does what he can to transform it to its artistic purpose. An older woman is similar to that wood, hard and obdurate in her denial at the onset of her recovery. The more yielding, the more receptive she becomes in her recovery, the more purposeful will she find herself to be.

As the older woman recovers and begins to rediscover herself, she may wish to follow the suggestion of therapist and writer Sam Keen, who hearkens back to Native American law as a notable code of behavior. When making an important decision or choice, Keen says, Native Americans consider how the consequences of their decision will affect the children of the seventh generation to follow. Think about it: what you do today will indeed affect all of our descendants. If we truly care about what happens to them, we shall have a healthy community, country and world. We will not be cutting down redwoods or allowing a tanker to spill the slightest drop of oil. We will be concerned about our forests and deserts and water and land. We will be building a better planet for our children to live in.

Anne

Sitting in a custom-made blue velvet wingback wheelchair in the lounge of a "cushy" private club, our designated meeting place halfway between her home and mine, was Anne. Her pink silk dress reached just above her knee and exposed one rolled-down nylon, knotted above her calf. A pink satin lap robe covered the space where the other leg ought to have been. She appeared at first to be fragile and weary, although determined to go through with the interview. Anne had something to say, her nurse told me coolly, or she would not have had the chauffeur drive them 200 miles to share her story with a perfect stranger.

Anne is 81, the daughter of two physicians who were owners of a string of nursing homes nearly a century ago. Anne's mother, of Norwegian descent and one of the first American female physicians, died of liver cancer when Anne was 31, one year after the family became aware of widespread, upper-crust gossip of her father's illicit liaison with the wife of a state senator. Anne began abusing alcohol soon after her mother's death.

> I simply could not find tears, I was so stunned and ashamed. I did not know the difference between grief and

dishonor. They came so close together, and in those days, to have cancer was shameful. So my father's infidelity and my mother's cancer were both grist for the gossip mill and stigmatic to our family name. I was treated as an outcast in our social circles.

Before my mother died, I was very well liked and social. But my father often told me I was too emotional and flighty. Sometimes he would tell me not to be so hysterical. When my mother died, I stopped showing all my feelings. And that was because I did not feel my feelings at all.

Anne's drug abuse began when she was 62, soon after her husband died, and she learned about the serenity that tranquilizers offered. At 69 she sought sobriety from all drugs and alcohol through the Hazelden treatment program and AA. At 75 her leg was amputated for bone cancer. She had been in remission now for eight years.

On this autumn day in the Midwest, she sat primly, looking me in the eye, her lips tight, her pale hands folded in her lap.

My granddaughter tells me you may be able to help me find out why my stepson insists on committing suicide.

She spoke graciously, refined and gentle, as if she might have been commenting on the design on the teacup sitting on the mahogany end table beside her.

He's been trying it all sorts of ways since he was a teenager . . . at least five times, and in different ways, some of them bloody. I'm afraid one of these days he'll fool us all and do the job. Tell me, do you believe this could be due to being brought up in an alcoholic family?

Anne refused my request to tape our interview, and she frequently punctuated her narrative with a warning gesture of her index finger, admonishing tactfully, "Don't write about that part." And I shall not.

We never did get around to finding out exactly why Sam wants to kill himself. But in that single afternoon we spent together, in the crisp, orange autumn of southern

Minnesota, I watched this lovely creature come to the realization that whatever Sam did was no longer her responsibility. I heard her story unfold and wondered if I was in a dream or seeing a great movie. I heard her conclusion, too: that probably she may have been a part of the cause of Sam's pain, but his healing from the family sickness was now *his* responsibility.

"I think I'll just have to turn it over," she said, and with a childlike gesture, her head tilted shyly toward me, she tossed back a wisp of white hair with a flick of her fingers.

As the story of her life's experiences began to take form, her voice rose and fell, her long thin hands reaching involuntarily, rhythmically, to her hair. The energy in the room spun upward as her emotions intensified. Like moths fluttering, her silver fingers removed the tiny white combs that held her immaculate hair high in snowy upsweep. Her passion was awesome. The anecdotes and tidbits of her narrative tumbled out, much like her long white hair, which now was cascading down over her shoulders. The combs dropped around her wheelchair like discarded worries. Once, in tears of memory, she looked down and exclaimed to the floor, somewhat startled and embarrassed, "Now look what I've done!" Then, as our eyes met, we laughed together in a delightful moment of unspoken recognition of the symbolism of her gestures.

As her laughter and her tears kept coming, Anne described the life of the rich and famous, the burden of being born into a family of scientists who were both intellectual and cosmopolitan, urbane and brittle, where graciousness meant perfection and ladylike meant practiced. Sexual promiscuity as a young woman had been her most well-kept secret, the one she believed to have been the reason she drank excessively in the beginning of her conscious self-recriminations. She spoke of affairs with family household employees, both men and women, with college men and her father's business associates. "I longed for love," she sighed, in a moment of self-forgiveness. "I was never held close as a child. The first time I can remember being told that someone loved me was in a riding stable in the straw, by a man I did not know."

When Anne left me at dusk, she was clear. While her servants prepared for her return to her limousine, we said good-bye. First she reached up and hugged me. Then returning to her more familiar world of cultivated decorum, she shook my hand with solemnity as one may in bidding farewell to a visiting ambassador. She had needed a stranger to hear her, she said, and now she was tired and wanted to go home to rest.

"Just tell them," she murmured, pointing to my notebook, "that it's never too late to find yourself. Tell them not to give up!"

I stood in the poplar-lined driveway as the black customized limousine glided imperiously out of sight, carrying Anne, self-created, a curious combination of pompous rigidity and liberated love, a venerable spirit of integrity. I, too, felt tired. And peaceful.

(Anne died on August 9, 1991. She bequeathed $500,000 to a fund established for the healing of women alcoholics.)

CHAPTER FOUR

Issues Of Recovery

A number of primary issues recurred throughout my interviews with older women recovering from co-dependence. A discussion of these issues follows here and in Chapter 5.

Discarding Traditions and Myth-Mandates

Important for older women in recovery is the conscious rejection of traditions that have long unconsciously entrapped them. Some must quit roles or jobs that have given them the little, yet oftentimes only, power they have felt in their families. These include, for example, the roles of "broadcaster" or "publisher" of family gossip, or "switchboard operator" to communication among family members. For many mothers relinquishing the pivotal position of "counselor mom" is anathema in early recovery. Not to be able to mediate among her offspring who are quarreling with each other seems at first an impossible task. But it is a very important one. Said 58-year-old Miriam:

> The most painful thing I ever had to do as a mother and recovering caretaker was to stand up in my living room in front of my six adult kids and tell them, "I have nothing left to give you." And as horrible as that sounded to me, I knew somewhere deep within me that it was healthy to say it.

The recovering older woman must let go of the importance of her reputation as a "good wife" or "good mother" and remain true to her own truth, what she defines as her own essential goodness. Said Samantha, 63 years old, recovering from what she described as "self-worth deprivation":

> The hardest part for me was learning I could love myself without having egomania, that self-esteem does not mean that I am lacking humility or that I am being grandiose or too big for my britches.

Many traditions are carried on in statements, attitudes and behaviors passed on to us at an early age and reinforced in our families and society as a whole. Unexamined, they assume the status of myths and, worse yet, gain power as mandates that must be followed in order for us to live correctly as the "good woman." The recovering older woman is in possession of many such myth-mandates that need examination and in many cases expunging. The following were described to me by older women interviewed for this book:

- You are not to talk about problems in the household and, for God's sake, at the same time be a good tattle-tale!
- Children are supposed to take care of parents when their parents get old.
- A good wife should be a good cook and homemaker and a selfless parent.

- A good mother sacrifices her time and energy and personal needs for the sake of her family.
- A good woman always looks like a lady. That is, she keeps her legs crossed, her hair done, her lipstick on straight and her slip doesn't show.
- A sweet little woman never complains or nags her husband. (Simple reminders are tantamount to nagging.)
- Husbands are always right or should be made to think they are.
- A woman should be honest at all times, but never so honest as to deflate her husband's ego.
- A good wife never goes to bed angry.
- Give your last cent to your family if they need it.
- A good wife is in charge of the couple's social life.
- Men should make more money to feel more powerful.
- All good parents love their children.
- All good women get married and live happily ever after.
- The man is supposed to be the boss.
- A good wife gives her husband sex when he wants it or he will get it somewhere else.
- The good woman's job is to fulfill the mandate given by her husband, the master. And then he will take care of her.
- Good women are ladylike. Ladylike means passive, inferior, agreeable and co-dependent.

Shame, Secrets And Shoulds

The older woman's three main points of connection to continuing dysfunction are shame, secrets and shoulds. They are her reasons for being, her family's and society's questionable gift to her.

For me the high price of serenity is the telling of all my secrets. Secrets cause shame, and shame in turn demands more secrets. To hide them both, we employ the use of shoulds. A woman's secret may be that her father beat her mother. She feels ashamed. She tells herself that she should not talk about it to anyone. Then, in a not unusual scenario she marries a man who beats her. Again, it is a shameful secret, the bruises of which she covers up by saying that she fell down the stairs.

One of my own most carefully guarded secrets is as old as my childhood: I never felt I belonged anywhere, not even with my family. This secret of mine is attached to ageist attitudes. The source of my shame: as a child, I was extremely embarrassed that my father was old enough to be my mother's father. This fact was so painful to me that I began to tell lies about my parents to strangers. Through fabrication and embellishment I was able to invent a more pleasing and acceptable picture of my family, the kind of family we "should" have been. By normalizing my family statistics I was able to feel that I belonged.

One of my interview subjects revealed her painful secret:

> My Al-Anon group [30 women] is filled with women whose biggest secret is their disappointment in their marriages . . . the failure of their spouses to keep their promise to "take care" of them and their children. One by one we have lost our big homes in Great Beach, and one by one we have been made to look at our "looking good" issue through coming upon each other working in drugstores and florist shops for $4.50 an hour. We're just too proud to admit we have no money, that our alcoholic husbands had failed. We've been listening to each other's excuses and rationalizations for why we're waiting tables or selling greeting cards in a novelty shop "just to keep busy." We've been lying to each other, lying to our own best friends! Now, that's really sick.

Secrets, shame and shoulds can kill us. One of my clients, 58-year-old Betty, was filled with them. I had begun to introduce her to the steps of co-dependent recovery as she was unable to remain abstinent from alcohol without addressing the caretaker issues that formed the core of her addictive behavior. One day she stomped out of my older women's group for Adult Children of

Alcoholics, yelling over her shoulder, "I don't want to look back. Let the dead bury the dead!" Today, Betty is dead. Unaddressed, unrevealed secrets fester and grow. They keep us from being honest with ourselves and intimate with others. Ultimately, they keep us trapped in our deadly dysfunction.

Dysfunctional families are filled with secrets. Many of them — Granddad couldn't read, Uncle Bob is gambling away his family's nest egg, Aunt Mary wasn't married when she got pregnant — are not obvious and must be pursued vigorously. Some we shall never learn — is it true that Great-great-grandpa abandoned a wife and family in Poland to start a new life, with a new wife, in America? — so complex and entrenched are they. Family secrets are nurtured until they have become part of the family's moral fiber, binding it together. Secrets become inculcated into the dysfunctional family's closed system and branded into each member's set of values as family policies, laws executed in the family through hierarchal competition and the ever-present threat of failure. The consequence of telling the secret is punishment by other family members, while the consequence of dutifully keeping the secret is a kind of enforced ignorance that is anything but blissful.

Dorothy, 70 years old, revealed to me that a big secret in her family was that she and her sisters were bulimic 50 years ago. She spoke with shame and anger about the "puke pit" in their backyard that all three sisters used when they were in high school so as not to gain pounds after enormous family dinners. Their parents were both weight-conscious. Demeaning their children verbally for being fat was used in their child-rearing as both punishment and threat. Today, all four of Dorothy's daughters are obese, carrying the weight, literally, of their mother's shame.

Another woman I interviewed talked about her husband who kept her informed for 25 years about his ongoing extramarital affairs. But when she had an affair of her own, he told her that infidelity was permissible for him but not for her. "Do you think I ever told my kids about any of that?" she asked me rhetorically. "Of course not. I always wanted them to think that their dad was a good guy. I never wanted to cause them the pain that they would experience if they knew what he had done. So I kept it a secret but after they were grown, they found out anyway. Then they went into therapy and were angry with me because I had taken out on them, through my stress and the strain of keeping the secret, the pain that I couldn't express."

Sometimes we keep a secret so masterfully that we hide it even from ourselves. We call this "freezing the guilting memory." An example involves two of my clients, Kathy and her mother. Kathy recalled an auto accident in which her father was driving drunk 33 years before, when she was five years old. When she cited this in a therapy session in her mother's presence, her mother expressed shock at her knowledge of the accident and disavowed that Kathy had even been present. But her daughter was able to describe graphic details of the accident, including the blood on the printed blouse that her mother had been wearing. Upon finally being convinced that Kathy had indeed been involved in the accident, her mother wept convulsively, crying, "My poor baby. I forgot. I'm so sorry. I didn't know."

As difficult as secrets are to live with, they are no less easy to reveal. Women more than men, notes alcoholism expert and author Marian Sandmaier in her book *The Invisible Alcoholics*, seem to have greater difficulty sharing their secrets. Because they fear that they will appear somehow unladylike, the process of revealing secrets is seen as more stigmatizing to women. But for the sake of our health, reveal them we must.

Following are some of the most well-kept secrets revealed to me by women I interviewed for this book:

- "I am smart."
- "I counseled and comforted my husband when he felt guilty while he was having an affair with another woman."

- "I wanted to be on the stage, but my stepfather jeered and said I'd be in the third row of the chorus. So I studied domestic science" (from a woman in London, age 70).
- "I hate cooking."
- "I became pregnant at my husband's insistence to keep him from having to go in to the army."
- "I love my children."
- "I love one of my children better than the others."
- "My biggest fear is that my husband will become ill and I will have to take care of him. So my secret is that I hope I die before he does."
- "I enjoyed the first orgasm of my life six years ago with my husband" (from an 80-year-old woman in recovery from alcoholism for nine years).
- "I was arrested for nudity at a beach in San Diego in 1935."
- "I ghostwrote most of my husband's books. He could not spell and his grammar was atrocious. In 1961 a publisher rejected a book that I wrote. Six months later we resubmitted the same manuscript under my husband's name, and it was accepted by the same publisher. It was all over for me after that" (from Marjorie, 77, in recovery from alcoholism and co-dependence for eight years and the widow of a famous author).
- "I wrote my husband's master's thesis."
- "Our family secret is that men are weak and women are strong."
- "Tuberculosis ran in my family."
- "I love my husband."
- "I am very angry."
- "Whenever I wanted to hear my husband tell me that he loved me, I would arrange for us to go to dinner and dancing. The only time he could tell me he loved me was when he whispered it in my ear in public on the dance floor" (from Frances, 81, a widow for 38 years, sober 16 years, who had her first drink after the death of her husband).

And examples of "shoulds" :

- "Siblings in our family are not supposed to support each other or our actions without some tacit approval from our mother."
- "I should never quit working."
- "I should avoid going to my bridge party this week because of my husband's drunken antics last time."
- "I should weigh 120 pounds."
- "I should know about art/politics/business/etc."
- "I'm a woman, so I should know how to hem a skirt, throw a dinner party and raise perfect children."
- "I should get up and make dinner for my husband even though I'm sick in bed with the flu."
- "I should always wear white on the tennis court."

Family Sainting

The stigma of aging is rooted primarily in our Western culture's fear of death. Death has become a bad word fraught with superstition. So fearsome is it that we can barely speak the word. Under the aegis of showing respect to the bereaved, we have installed numerous euphemisms to render death more palatable, such as the Grim Reaper, the Pale Horse, Crossing the Bar, Passed, Passed On, Passed Away, In Heaven, Just Away and Asleep.

Since fear in our society denotes negativity and weakness, not talking about fearsome death has become a national norm. Death is as taboo in the 1990s as sex was in the 1930s. Aging and dying are certainly not topics of conversation in the average household. In a moment of reverie we may envision our great aunts and uncles passing through the pearly gates and rocking and chatting on that celestial front porch, but rarely do we see ourselves or those dearest to us joining them. Little wonder, then, given this situation, that members of today's younger generation choose not to feel too strongly about their mothers or fathers since every wrinkle and grey hair remind them of the unthinkable. In our analgesic society we will go to nearly any end to avoid pain, including that of rejecting intimacy with those who threaten to cause us pain by dying, thus triggering our fear of abandonment.

Death is further perverted in the dictum, well-rehearsed by the dysfunctional family, that the ancestral dead, if spoken of at all, are spoken of with reverence. Sometimes this comes very easily. There are those family heroes who have left this planet as proud soldiers in the glory of a war and so have, of course, gone sailing on to heaven. They have ceased in our minds to embody any human frailties or vulnerabilities and have assumed the status of saints by the time they become topics of dinner conversation. Elevating other family members to this lofty level may require a bit more effort, but in the dysfunctional family, not much more.

Family sainting in such families generally takes about as long as it takes to bury the body or to dispose of the ashes. The frequency and level of beatification of family sainthood are in direct proportion to the level of loyalty that family members felt for the deceased — even in the face of evidence that loyalty may not have been deserved. Uncle Joe may have drunk too much or beaten his wife or spent time behind bars for embezzlement, but once he is dead he is transformed to Saint Joe, the jolly old uncle who bought his wife roses and the kids new toys to make up for getting "a little tipsy" the night before. Reality takes a backseat to denial. Certainly Grandma and Grandpa could not have been abusive, goes the family lore, for Grandpa was a hero during the war and Grandma won first place with her lone-star quilt.

We simply are not to talk disrespectfully about the dead. One of my interview subjects, a widow named Eleanor, had been married to an alcoholic and a chronic childbeater. When he died, she told me, her children stood up at the memorial service and talked about what a wonderful father he was. Eleanor found herself feeling better, thinking that perhaps they had forgotten how physically cruel he had been. She felt relieved of guilt for choosing a mate who was so abusive to both her and her children. From that point on, until she began her recovery from co-dependence, she went into a kind of amnesia, or trance, during which she actually believed that all the harm he had done had not really happened.

Entire families are known to block out the abuse from their consciousness. This serves two purposes: the family members can avoid dealing with the pain they carry, and they can continue to be proud of their family heritage. They do not have to admit that theirs may have been a family that they can no longer boast about. But before we blame them, let us remember that this is just another form of denial, called repression, that comes with the disease of co-dependence. Such a family is not lacking in dignity but lacking in health. Said Eleanor:

> It was only when I discovered my grandkids were getting the same kind of brutal treatment from their fathers that my husband had given them that I decided I'd better learn something about my own part in the abuse to my kids. That's when I went into treatment, and my own kids were called in for family sessions, and now everybody's in treatment. It is painful, but my grandchildren are not going to be abused again, and I'm hoping they'll grow up to be healthy parents. We're all trying.

Myths about family saints are passed along to us as children in our families of dysfunction. We grow up believing lies. In many households dead perpetrators of physical or emotional battering or even incest are blameless by mere virtue of the fact that they are dead. It becomes the distorted reality of their descendants, then, that any impurities in the family could only have been spontaneously generated in the present. We, the living, are pinned with full responsibility for whatever problems manifest themselves in our lives, from drug abuse to wrecked marriages, even though the patterns of such difficulties may have been in formation generations ago.

In our recovery we must challenge the status of family saints, peering beneath their glowing aura to the true essence of their existence. The family secrets that many of these people took to their death are valuable items of family history, information that we may make use of in our own lives for understanding, intervening in and preventing disease. Some families may label discussion of these secrets as shameful family gossip. But this is anything but gossip. This is a search for truth. In the same way that physicians seek their patients' family history of cancer, heart disease or diabetes in order to be forewarned of potential disease, it is beneficial for descendants of the deceased to discuss the person honestly in order to trace patterns that are passed down genetically and through family socialization.

Genealogical Charts

Knowing the truth about family saints also proves useful in resolving harmful family conflicts. Many a funeral hymn has been sung with dark clouds of disharmony gathering in the dissident distance. To speak candidly of family quarrels is considered heresy in some families, but this is the route to resolving once and for all unfinished business between the deceased and the survivors.

Genealogical charts, including emotional family trees, are a very helpful tool for deciphering the pain passed down by family saints. I suggest to most of my clients that they do their own genealogical chart.

To do one yourself, on a large piece of paper chart information regarding family members, tracing back at least to your grandparents or further if you can remember or can gather information.

This is not strictly a factual chart. You need to present wherever possible such demographic data as each person's name, sex, date of birth and date and cause of death. But this family tree also traces emotions. Include yourself in the chart at whatever age you would like to be, then place your relatives and significant others close to you or at a distance, depending on how you experienced them emotionally. While you're at it, write one or two of your feeling adjectives — affectionate, angry, depressed, optimistic, etc. — beside the name of each family member. In this way you will be better able to determine those persons in your family, living or dead, with whom you still carry unresolved issues.

Interestingly, despite the doggedness with which many families hide their secrets, most are quite willing to reveal factual information if they view doing so as an assignment. This is one way, in fact, that mothers can help their children in recovery, by revealing the family secrets.

The Alcoholic And Abusive Marriage

One question I asked during my interviews for this book was, "What were the most painful years of your life?" Distressingly, literally dozens of women said that those were the years when they were married to alcoholic and abusive husbands. They continued to stay with those husbands, they said, because doing so was better than the feared alternative: poverty and the inability to sustain their lives and the lives of their children. Some of these women talked about having been physically battered and having their lives threatened. The choice to leave sometimes was available and was considered, but they chose to stay. And for all those years, they felt they were in prison.

Today many of these women in recovery are now divorced or their husbands dead and they feel great relief. But now they must deal with the offspring of those abusive marriages, their adult children who are now very angry that their mothers stayed with their fathers. These women are in a no-win situation. They lingered in the abuse, they believe, to save their children's lives, but now their children are angry at them for having done just that.

In some cases children of such marriages are angry and confused because their parents divorced. This often results, we find, when the mother had been secretive, hiding from her children the truth about her husband's abuse. These children had little understanding of their mother's sordid plight or the degree of her powerlessness. Many

women protected their husbands no matter what the repercussions. Said one such woman to me, "I think the
children have the right to respect their father regardless
of the circumstances."

Other statements of misplaced loyalty by women I interviewed were quite illustrative of the kinds of attitudes that
proliferate in chronically abusive relationships. Among them
are these revelations, which some recovering women discovered about themselves:

- "It is familiar for me to think of myself as inferior."
- "I am comfortable with bad treatment."
- "I am not comfortable without an oppressive partner."
- "I have been taught that all criticism is true . . . and
  the best way to avoid criticism is to do it to others
  before they do it to me."
- "Compliments are not to be trusted. I was taught that
  giving compliments to others, however sincere, was
  not safe."
- "Here I am, 10 years after my divorce, still wanting to
  hear through my daughters whether or not my former
  abusive husband inquires about me or my well-being."

Abuse covers a wide range of behaviors, all of them
harmful. Emotional downgrading of the sort Loretta, 57,
described, is one variety: "Now I know he really did not
believe he would ever be successful, and we set it up so
I could be blamed for his failure . . . That became the
whole script."

The emotional abuse that an actively alcoholic husband
is capable of heaping upon his wife can be deadening.
When such a wife is asked what she feels about her husband and she replies that it is not love but is too painful
for her to describe — but she cannot leave him — she is
a battered woman. At the extreme end of the scale of
abuse is black-eyed, broken-limbed, life-threatening physical battering.

Many women in dysfunction feel comfortable only
when they experience the abuse. This ironically is the

only time they feel safe. When they are in the center of the abuse, they know where they are, and they experience a sense of false control. Being in the middle of it feels better, or less dangerous, than the expectation and fear of it.

Clients will sometimes ask me, "Do I have to leave my husband if he's alcoholic or abusive?" I tell them that the decision is theirs. They have to make a choice about whether or not they want to deal with the situation without having to change or fix their husbands because they are powerless to change or fix him. They have power only in their choices and their own recovery. The woman who chooses her own recovery eventually will need to address her abusive marriage. As one of my clients, Lydia, 55, said: "I know that ultimately I will have to leave him or he will have to get out because the healthier I get, the less willing I am to tolerate his illness. It is unimaginable. I will not live with someone who is this sick."

Many alcoholic men leave their wives, often for younger women. This is common in our culture. Yet as the older women who have been abandoned recover from their co-dependence, not a few have told me something like, "I would like to ask that woman he went to if she'd like me to take him back, and then I would tell her that I don't want him back. I'd like to say to her, 'I'm glad you've got him because I didn't realize what a mess I was in until I was free of him, until I began to realize that he is not my Higher Power.' I can take care of myself."

A physically battered woman who tells herself every day that tomorrow she will leave — or after Joey's birthday or after the family reunion or after her youngest daughter graduates — is only fooling herself. She is deluding herself into believing that things will change. Maybe she will get a better job and won't have to leave. Maybe problems will no longer be her fault, and she can remain with him. Maybe he will stop hitting her if this time she does everything perfectly.

Every battered woman who stays in the situation does so to try to gain validation from the very person who has robbed her of that validation and who has confiscated her identity. This is addiction. This is denial. She believes that she deserves nothing better than what she has. She rarely knows that she is living in a battering environment. Tragically until she is willing to pull herself from a situation in which she is drowning, she is not even aware that she is drowning. Not until she crawls out of the ocean does she realize she is exhausted, cold and sopping wet. To that woman, I would like to say, come out of the icy water now and thaw out in the sun. You will be safer in the sun.

Sexual Issues

Recovering older women have numerous and complex issues related to sexuality. Some women view the manipulation of sex as a means of getting what they want. Said Elisabet, 56, from Germany:

> I do not love my husband. In fact I hate him . . . My husband is a perfectionist and a pain in the neck. I am gentle in bed, and he is no longer impotent, as he was when I married him. I have to put up with him until August, when I get my doctoral degree. Then I will be able to support myself. My gentleness in bed is my only leverage with my husband. Sometimes I feel like I'm selling myself, but I am also a survivor of World War II. I have received a medal from the German government. I am respected. I have had a hard time.

Also problematic, many women who need and yearn for connection with others are willing to be sexual in order to satisfy that need. They believe that being sexual presents the only opportunity to feel loved. If a woman did not receive nurture — even in the form of a simple hug — as a child or in her intimate relationships as a young adult, she finds it all but impossible to accept nurture as an older woman. In my therapy groups women who have the most difficulty receiving hugs are those who have neither children nor close relationships with women.

One of the most defective beliefs of our culture is that love equals sex. The demonstration of love through simple touching is thought to be and is feared as sexual. Nurturance, however, is not sexual. While it is often the case in an intimate relationship that nurturance and sex can be complementary, increasing pleasure and manifesting love, they do not in all cases accompany one another and surely are not synonymous.

Many women in the beginning of recovery are uncomfortable with hugs from other females because they fear they may be regarded as or may become lesbian. The name for this is homophobia, the internalized hatred and fear of same-gender love. Women who have suffered sexual and/or other violent physical abuse also have difficulty with the physical closeness that nurturance provides. This is a significant problem for recovering women suffering from the psychological and physical repercussions of sexual abuse by men, sometimes even by their own fathers. Recalled Florence, 69, who lives on a farm near Dubuque, Iowa:

> When I was a child, my mother and the mother of the kids on the farm bordering our farm took turns watching all of us kids, to keep our dads from molesting us when our mothers were away grocery shopping. We all knew it. All the kids used to refer to it as "our German dads with the Roman hands" . . . but some of us girls got caught [by our fathers] anyway, and I carried my pain about that around with me through two marriages and seven children, all by myself. It wasn't until Al-Anon that I started really talking about it. I was really suicidal and afraid of old age. At my Al-Anon meeting I found out about a women's group held at the battered women's shelter in Dubuque. It was a safe place I could talk about myself, and I found out I wasn't such a bad person. That is where I found my first friends as an adult. That really saved my life.

Sexual abuse is a core issue found frequently in both chemical dependence and co-dependence. It has been going on for generations. Dealing with its scars is an essential part of recovery, as many women have discovered:

I decided I was not going to my grave without telling somebody how much I wanted all my life to kill my incesting father. I came close to killing myself first, though, through alcohol. But when I felt validated in an Incest Survivors Anonymous (ISA) group in Chicago, that felt so good I decided to start going to Alcoholics Anonymous. I've been sober for two years now, and I also came out of the closet as a lesbian. I wish I had been out as a lesbian when my lover died ten years ago. We were lovers for 20 years. When she died, I had no one to talk to at work or anywhere. Our families had ousted us when we got together, so I couldn't talk to my sisters or brother about how I felt. I just buried all my stuff until now. I have more friends now than I have ever had in my life. I only wish I'd made things a lot easier for myself and come out of the closet 20 years ago.

Would this speaker, Lonnie, 66, advise other closeted older lesbians to share their sexual orientation now, I asked. "Absolutely," she replied emphatically. "It's never too late to find out you're a good person, regardless of who you choose to have as your life's partner."

CHAPTER FIVE

Anger And Other Issues Of Recovery

Recently I was listening to a call-in radio show. The two male guests were disagreeing with each other. The discussion between them became quite heated, about which the male moderator remarked, "We certainly have some spirited and challenging conversation here." When a woman called in to express her own divergent views, however, the moderator said, "We've really got some *angry* people calling in."

The woman caller, to my mind, was no angrier than the men, and perhaps even less so. What this exchange demonstrated was the double standard society offers to men and women regarding appropriate emotional expression.

Women are fearful of being called angry. We are sitting ducks for such an accusation. Any woman who dares to examine and criticize an existing injustice in our society is frequently labeled "a very angry woman." I remember that when Anne W. Schaef's book *Women's Reality* was first published, some socially unaware mental healthcare workers referred to her as "such an angry woman." When Virginia Hoffman wrote her book *Birthing a Living Church* in which she stated her belief that the Catholic Church no longer needed priests, I heard a priest scathingly suggest from his pulpit that Hoffman was "a very angry woman." Such blaming without honoring her analysis, without even acknowledging the points of her argument, is an example of disrespect and, in the milieu of formal debate, irresponsible. It is but one method used to keep quiet the rich tones of righteous anger. And it is applied again and again to women, especially older women, who have been expected to be passive and cooperative all their lives.

We shall remain a sexist society until women's anger is embraced as valid, righteous, worthy and healthy. By definition the recovering older woman is also an angry woman. We have lived our lives oppressed, although we are taught that oppression is neither just nor healthy. We are further oppressed by the oft-stated idea that women are as responsible for their oppression as men are. Real equality between the sexes, this line of thinking goes, is not really desirable to women.

Nothing could be farther from the truth. As recovering older women progressing in our newfound health, we demand an end to women's oppression. As they say, we're mad as hell and won't take it anymore.

What are we angry about? So many things:

> All those years when I was angry most of the time and sick the rest of it, I thought it was PMS. Later I was told by my psychiatrist that I was probably angry because I was going through "the change." Now I know it may have been partly that, but mostly I was angry because my father was an alcoholic. I've also noticed that my own daughters save their anger until they are premenstrual and then fling out their rage. I did the same thing. Being premenstrual

was more acceptable than being angry. But it doesn't work, anyway, because in the corporate world, men do not hire women who have a history of PMS. "On the rag" is not a reason to be absent or angry is what my husband used to say.

Millie tells her story:

I was told I was special because I was a girl. I was always told that I was the special one. But it was my brother who got a room of his own, a car of his own, who went to a special school and on to college. I was told to go to the corner and play with my dolls. I wasn't cared about. I had to figure out what they needed, and I didn't fit into their system because their system always changed, and I never did it right. Even now, at 57, when I go to visit them and take food to them, my father says, "Oh, don't bring that garbage in here." The "garbage" was a turkey that I got up at 4:00 A.M. to prepare and drive 160 miles to deliver. I am still trying. Is that sick or what?

My father is bitter and hateful and he abuses my mother. She never protected me. When I was 12 and my cousin, who lived upstairs and was 10 years older than me, tried to rape me in the front hall when I came home from school, my mother shushed me, admonished me to be quiet about it and to come home after that through the back door where he couldn't see me. Now I remember it and I am furious!

We are angry at our past and present circumstances, at people, places and things of every sort. And we are angry that as older women we are not supposed to be angry. In our culture there is no safe place for a woman to put her anger without suffering a residue of guilt for having done so. Even 12-Step groups have trouble with anger. A common notion is that the Big Book of Alcoholics Anonymous implores us not to have anger. But this is a misinterpretation. The Big Book does not deny us anger, but rather admonishes us not to hang on to it.

The fact is every one of us is going to experience anger, a natural human emotion. In recovery we must ferret out the source of our rage and then direct it appropriately, thereby freeing ourselves of it. Many older women are for the very first time acknowledging that they suffered emotional, physical and sexual abuse during their childhoods. Finally they are expressing the rage and hurt that they have been carrying around for the many long decades that they have lived.

No small amount of an older woman's anger, incidentally, is directed toward herself for mistakes she made as a mother. She bore the primary responsibility of child-rearing and today bears the brunt of blame by unhappy and dysfunctional children. Essential to her recovery is the recognition that she, like most mothers, followed the path of parenting that she learned from her own parents.

The Dangers Of Unexpressed Anger

We must feel our anger, and we must express it. We cannot effectively think or talk away anger. Talking about anger merely cites its presence. It does little to reduce it. We must express it.

The consequences of failing to express anger in healthy ways are serious. If we do not reduce our rage, we are likely to become physically ill. The inability of women to express their anger accounts at least in part, I believe, for the high correlation in this country between women recovering from alcoholism and suffering from breast cancer. These women have no place to direct the anger that naturally emerges as they clear themselves of the addictive substances with which they suppressed their feelings. Unexpressed anger is internalized and becomes manifest in the most vulnerable and significant organ of nurturance, our breasts.

Unexpressed anger often emerges sideways or indirectly. For example, if an alcoholic woman bearing such a burden is a mother, she may heap her rage upon her children. Yelling, yanking, pinching, hitting — such acts of violence against those less powerful than herself are common behaviors in the alcoholic or chemically dependent mother.

But even should she become abstinent and is ostensibly sober, her rage may mount, becoming even more pervasive until she learns to express her rage appropriately and that means in a safe place. This is the point at which she needs to address her co-dependent issues.

Unexpressed anger works its way out in other round-about ways. One of them is in such passive-aggressive behaviors as feigning unawareness or being chronically tardy. One of my clients is habitually late to her group therapy sessions, angrily flouting unacceptable behavior that is unfair to the others, to me and is irresponsible to herself. Another indirect route is sarcasm: rather than state her feelings directly, the angry person dances around in a pointed, witty, sophisticated manner designed to disturb her audience. We see entire families resorting to sarcasm as a way to dispel pain and find comfort. When "I was just kidding" becomes a family slogan, you can count on sarcasm signaling rage at the core of family communication.

Gossip

One of the more acrimonious customs used to express anger indirectly is gossip. A devious drama in which stories, true and untrue, told by one person to another resulting in the contamination of a third person's reputation, gossip is common where direct communication is difficult and conflicts remain unresolved for long periods of time, if not forever. Family gossip serves to release some of the pressure-cooker discomfort of anger by making someone else appear bad or wrong while the person doing the gossiping gets to feel good and important, however briefly.

Gossip is a significant issue for the older woman. It obeys the cardinal rule that holds that she should never let the person she is angry with know that she is angry. Through gossip, however, she is allowed to let others know she is indeed angry and exactly why, thus providing a vent for her anger. So gossip serves a useful purpose for her, although it is injurious to all concerned, including herself, for gossip cunningly erodes one's self-esteem.

Complicating the issue are some of the more subtle, but no less harmful, ways in which we gossip. One of these is to couch discussion about another person in what appears to be concern: "I worry about Jill because she stays out all night with a married man and doesn't get enough rest," or "I worry about my two brothers because one is trying to steal land from the other."

Another approach is to pity, making a judgment about someone by "feeling sorry" for her: "I feel sorry for my sister because she is a hypochondriac and is having problems with her boss because of all the sick days she takes." Under the aegis of worry and pity, the toxic information is effectively carried on its way, and the subject of the gossip is blamed for the worrisome or pitiful situation.

Unlike family storytelling, a way of relating family lore and generational history in a loving manner, gossip is divisive, depreciating, corrosive, deceitful and degenerative to relationships. In recovery we eschew the practice of it.

Expressing Anger

A significant number of my clients have difficulty expressing anger. Many women feel that if they get angry, there will be no stopping it. Let me note that I have never seen this happen. Anger's expression always ends. There is always a start and a finish. Of course all healthy human beings will have anger at various times during their lives. This ought not to have shame attached to it. It is our responsibility to deal with our anger appropriately, as we feel it.

Another problem is that many women, when they finally find their anger, feel absolutely outraged and fairly fly in the face of all the injustices they have suffered. About 20 seconds after their outburst, however, they are overcome with guilt for feeling this way. With practice in expressing anger, guilt ceases to rise as an instant reaction.

My clients find a number of practical techniques useful for feeling and then dealing with anger. One of them begins with making a list of people and things that you would be angry about if you could be angry. Next, have a dialogue with each of them, one by one. You may do this silently to yourself. You may write it out on a piece of paper or in a journal. You may very well want to get more physical. I suggest using an old tennis racket to pound on your bed, or close your windows and scream. Some of my clients write words describing their anger on rocks. Then they throw the rocks in a lake, screaming their anger as they hurl the rocks to their watery depths. This way of letting go has received remarkably high ratings!

Artwork may help. Some of my clients use crayons or paint to articulate their anger visually, expressing their rage in an explosion of color. Some use visualization as a device to reduce their perpetrators to tiny, helpless figures. Many techniques exist that may help you, first to feel your anger and then to express it, expel it, eject it, release it. Do not hold it inside. Anger is toxic if you do not express it.

Accepting Confrontation

You and I are not the only people who get angry. Sometimes other people will be angry with us. When we are in recovery, we are saying that we are willing to accept confrontation by another person. We are willing to receive another person's reality, as painful as that may be. Very often confrontation feels like abuse, like old times in our abusive families. As a result we may react as we did when we were children. We may run away from the confronter. We may cry victim. Or we may get angry and hit back.

In recovery we learn not to react abruptly, but rather to respond thoughtfully. If, for instance, we are told that we are being abrupt or invasive or not acceptable to others, rather than reacting defensively, we need to hear what this person is saying. We need to respect what is being said as someone's reality, and we need to process the information. We need to go inside ourselves and consider carefully whether or not what they are saying does indeed fit, whether or not their interpretation is accurate. It is possible that we may determine that they are off base, that the way we are is healthy and that we do not need to change. But if the confronter is on target, we need to honor this new awareness from our perspective as a healthy, responsible adult. We need to say, yes, you're right, I own this. Doing so requires humility and a willingness to change. It may seem simple, but it is not easy. We must be willing to practice and so, slowly, shall we learn.

I cite an example from my own life that occurred during a visit not long ago with one of my nieces. I learned that this young woman in her 30s is sometimes frightened of me because of what she interprets as my anger. I was quite shocked upon hearing this. I had not perceived myself as either feeling anger or behaving angrily with her. In listening to what she had to say and in viewing my own behavior with as much objectivity as I could summon, I discovered that what she experienced as my anger was very likely impatience, which is certainly a form of anger and control.

Truth be told, I had to admit that I did at times feel impatient with others who did not comprehend immediately what I was attempting to communicate. At these times my audience was treated to a rolling of my eyes while I simultaneously uttered irritating *tsk* sounds. Having had this realization, I had to own my impatience. My niece and I were able to come to an agreement: if she feels that I am being impatient, she is to give me a signal to alert me. Meanwhile I have begun to practice consciously being patient and accepting of others.

I am grateful to my niece for her risk-taking. No one had ever before brought this objectionable behavior to my attention. Yet only a fearless inventory of my behavior suggested the veracity of her experience. In this way we have both benefited from her honest confrontation.

Premature Forgiveness: A Danger Signal

It can safely be said that as older women we feel anger toward numerous people, perpetrators, situations and institutions. Traditionally we have been told that forgiveness is essential to healing. Forgiveness, however, is the icing on the cake, not the cake itself.

It is paramount that we distinguish between those perpetrators who *knew* they were inflicting pain on us and yet continued to perpetrate and those who were ignorant of the consequences of their actions. This process enables us to sort out those who we may decide to remain unforgiving toward and those who we shall forgive. We are fully able to heal from our aggressors' perpetrations of pain without forgiveness. Perhaps it will come when we have expressed our anger toward them and perhaps not.

A real danger is "deciding" to forgive. If forgiveness happens and we feel it, we are blessed. But we cannot make it happen, although we may say "I forgive you" a hundred times. Premature forgiveness or forgiveness that is exercised as a result of conscious, intellectualized choice before the emotional healing process is completed can be threatening to our health. It is a killer of unrecovering co-dependents. If anger and grief are not expressed and released from the body, physical illness manifests. Forgiving prematurely is tantamount to saying, "Here, take another breast, remove my womb, give me cancer." As one of my teachers said, "What the mind doesn't tell us, our bodies will."

Premature forgiveness is especially common among older women. All our lives we have been urged by society to forgive and forget, linking this practice with the virtuous life. In a culture in which women's oppression and a losing struggle for parity prevail, forgiveness of the aggressor or perpetrator is necessary for the continuation of the regime. Standing firm against this social dictum is an abiding challenge.

Self-Forgiveness

Much more important than being able to forgive others is being able to forgive ourselves. We older women, especially those longtime caretakers among us, have generally accumulated quite a long list of characteristics about which we can be unforgiving toward ourselves, from disgust at the way we behaved in public while drunk to our inability to perform any task perfectly. Becoming the prime target of our own unrelenting rage, we direct our anger inward and become depressed.

A major task of recovery for many older mothers is acknowledging and forgiving themselves for their abusive behavior toward their children. Such abuse was likely to have escalated during their recovery from chemical dependence but continued in their co-dependence.

So painful can it be to face this that many women in recovery deny that any such behavior occurred. I have had the experience of working with a mother and daughter together in the same room, the mother shaking her head in denial while the daughter adamantly asserting, "Yes, Mother, you did, too. . . . You did so begin hitting me more often nine years ago, after you stopped drinking. That's when the beatings really got bad. Mother, you broke your high-heeled shoe on my back, remember?"

My clients have related countless stories about Ping-Pong paddles, fraternity paddles, wooden spoons, even two-by-fours being broken over their hindsides. Such allegations are very painful for healing mothers to hear. Most of them do not remember the specific incidents that their offspring recall so vividly from their childhoods. The "white-out" system is hard at work: the perpetrator is frequently without memory and must be reminded. It takes time for her to admit that these fits of outrage possibly could have occurred at all, let alone that she was the perpetrator. Even after her memory has been jogged, admitting to violent behavior is extremely onerous to the recovering mother for it is in direct opposition to her values as a woman.

Further, to admit that she was physically violent during her recovery from chemical dependence is anathema to the recovering woman. To acknowledge these violent behaviors, she must once more visit that place of unresolved pain where she resided in those first trying days when she was without her alcohol or drugs. This part of the healing process is long and extremely trying.

As one of my clients, slowly cutting through her co-dependence, stated, "I find I must now change my attitude toward my parenting when my children were younger and I was so unhappy. What I believed to be just a little tap on my kids' hindsides was in reality violence. Now I must own that I am a recovering child abuser. This may be too hard for me ever to do."

This is a pivotal and precarious point in a woman's recovery. It becomes crucial that she have a safe place to bleed off her guilt — in therapy, with a sponsor in her 12-Step program, with a trusted friend. If we feel judged for our behaviors, especially if we suffer from being overly concerned about how others view us, we may never be able to forgive ourselves. It is here that AA's Eighth and Ninth steps — making a list of people we had harmed and making amends to them — become useful. It now becomes paramount that we put the blame where it belongs, on the disease, on the dysfunction. This does not mean, however, that we don't need to take responsibility for the damage we have done and for changing our patterns of destructive behavior. Recovery demands that we have the willingness to change ourselves.

In these ways we can finally begin to view ourselves with dignity and respect, as having a disease from which we are thankfully recovering.

Assertiveness

Assertiveness, once again, is the art of getting what we need and want without having to hurt others or ourselves. This may sound simple enough, and mention has

been made of it earlier in this book. However, assertiveness as a need merits an echo because many women,
especially older women, experience enormous difficulty
in this area. It has been our wont, after all, to be passive,
aggressive and passive-aggressive. As we observe others
achieving and attaining, reaching their goals, we keep
hoping that then perhaps we can get, however miraculously, what we want, too. Actually things have never
quite worked out this smoothly. Our needs and wants,
our healthy human desires, do assert themselves despite
our sick attempts at suppression and sublimation. But
because we are not supposed to acknowledge them, let
alone do something about them, we have developed indirect ways of fulfilling these needs.

Many older women have become masters of manipulation. Perhaps they withhold sexual favors from their husbands until they get them to agree to help with the housework. Some women threaten their children with white
violence, a deadly, nerve-wracking silence that prompts the
kids to clean their rooms just so Mom will talk to them
again. Many women resort to raging outbursts (releases
of stockpiled anger) or acts of violence, simply taking what
they want through a show of force.

The cry-wolf approach, in which a woman's needs must
be expressed through a crisis, is demonstrated in Susan,
a mother of five and the spouse of an active alcoholic. She
is overwrought, overworked, self-loathing and angry. She
would like a Saturday afternoon away from her family,
she yells, to take a solitary drive to an art fair out in the
country. Rather than state her desire directly, however,
she complains to her family at great martyrish length on
Saturday morning about how she is "sick and tired" of
spending every weekend cooking and cleaning for them,
how they are driving her crazy and why she absolutely
has to be by herself — all of this delivered with dramatic
tears and hand-wringing. Finally she jumps into the car
and races off to the art fair — an outcome that, in recovery, could have been realized simply by stating her needs
and making healthy choices.

These indirect approaches have generally been the acceptable way in which women have attained what they want in a society in which youth and violence have the prevailing power. Sexual wiles and social guile have served us in obtaining everything from material goods to a sense of self-worth. Or so it seems. In recovery, the older woman finally learns to deal more directly with her wants and needs. The aging woman, as she practices direct communication, will encounter compromising and subjugating attitudes all around her, among public servants, storekeepers, employers and in her family as well. She needs to discern which doors to knock on, whom she can trust among lawyers and accountants, doctors and clergy, friends and family to get her desires satisfied.

It was through assertiveness, for example, that my 56-year-old client, Mary, was finally able to tell her dictatorial 78-year-old father that his job of parenting her is over, that they may be friends but that he is no longer her authority figure. "I care about you, I love you, we have a long history together and I want to be your friend," Mary finally told him. "But I will not any longer subject myself to your verbal or emotional abuse, to your authoritarian gestures and attitudes."

Mary's father quit smoking cigarettes 20 years ago and took up a pipe, and when Mary began her own valiant struggle to quit smoking, her father insisted on telling her how to stop smoking cigarettes. Mary finally was able to say to him, "Don't tell me about how to quit smoking. You're still smoking. You've just substituted a pipe for cigarettes in your nicotine addiction." Mary exulted in her next group therapy session: "For the first time in my whole life, my dad backed off! Of course, it was the first time I had ever contradicted him, too, and my legs were shaking." At another point Mary's father told her how she should feel about something, and she retorted that he had no right to tell her how to feel. Again, he relented. With every act of assertion, Mary becomes more empowered, more self-confident.

Every older woman needs to be as clear as possible about what she wants and needs. She needs to state it, write it down or in some cases get assistance from a relative, social worker or other professional. (For more on this, see Chapter 8 and the Addendum.)

A number of techniques have been developed to help women become more assertive. One of the most effective ones is the broken-record technique, in which a woman repeats again and again what she wants in the same words and voice inflection. This effectively cuts through others' objections and obfuscations.

An incident from my own life provides an example. I wanted to buy a specific kind of insurance. The agent, however, kept trying to sell me something else. Knowing what I wanted, I simply kept repeating it until I got it. I have had to do the same when buying a certain kind of car or dress, even in negotiating salary. This technique is especially workable for older women, who have in the past been easy prey for people who would like to sell them something other than what they want. Form a clear simple statement of what you want, keep saying it and eventually you will get it.

Some women benefit from taking a class or workshop on assertiveness techniques. My clients often practice assertiveness without being combative or contentious in our therapy groups before taking it to the outside world. They are not always successful the first few times. I am reminded of one client who was very sturdy, adamant and assertive in her therapy group, but who in the presence of her daughter reverted to a puttylike chameleon, unable to make choices and decisions for herself. Many weeks passed as she voiced her own needs again and again in the presence of her daughter before she was finally heard.

One of the best first steps to assertiveness is self-affirmation, a powerful way to alter your very attitude: tell yourself, "I have a perfect right to what I need and want. Because of this I am a healthy woman."

Money

A monumental issue surfaced during the course of my interviews for this book: the global difficulty that older women have in dealing with money. In pinpointing sources of shame and the secrets in the families of origin of the women with whom I spoke, we delved into matters of money, past and present.

"Who paid the bills?" I asked them. "What kind of money, if any, did you handle and were you given an allowance?" "Was your mother's name on the family's checks?" Very rarely was this the case. Both the older woman interviewed and her mother usually had to ask their husbands for a check or tell them that they needed them to sign a number of checks to enable them to pay bills. In effect the women would have to defer to the men, ask them for money.

This subservience and lack of freedom became a source of shame for the interviewees. Most did not or do not have access to the family funds. Most have to request household money from their husbands. Some simply have to ask, some have to beg. Some of them told me that rather than ask for money to buy clothing and other personal items, they buy these necessities out of the household money. This, they said, required scrimping and saving. Some women hide little stashes of cash around the house in places their husbands don't know about. In some cases this comprised their only personal financial resource.

And so in the financial arena we find the generational chain of dependence most blatant. A woman's husband may forever be telling her that all he wants is for her to be happy, that she doesn't need to work, not even to cook or clean or sew. He wants to give her, he says, all the freedom she wants. He may even have her name printed on his checks. But still she has to ask him to pull a check out of his book when she needs money. Then comes the part when he accuses her of overspending but refuses to show her his bank statement because, he jokes, his bookkeeping cannot bear close scrutiny. Ultimately he is in absolute control.

Having an allowance of money from their husbands is viewed by many older women as a given for women in our patriarchal society. Many older women have resigned themselves to their plight rather than confront the predictable impatience, disgust or anger displayed by spouses. So accustomed are women to this inequity, this oppression, that they are not even aware of the depreciation that comes with having to beg for what they rightfully earn, those resources to which they have a perfect right as an adult partner. "He's always handled the checkbook," says Marge. "I just have never considered I had a right to touch it."

Lisa was a client who had been having a great deal of difficulty continuing her 30-year marriage. Her spouse, John, accompanied her to therapy very willingly over a six-month period. What we discovered was that unresolved issues with her father led Lisa to look to John to parent her, and John was not willing to fulfill that role. He was very opposed to the idea of playing Lisa's daddy. And yet he gave her a meager allowance every two weeks. Here was a man who earned $300,000 a year as a managing partner of a large firm, yet he was virtually unconscious about the realities of his family's own finances. Lisa could barely eke out enough for food from the pittance that he gave her.

John was not, however, an ungenerous man. Further investigation disclosed that both he and Lisa came from the Great Depression. His background was one of poverty among urban immigrants who had little money. As a result, today he has a slightly skewed idea of what money is about, not to mention a slightly skewed idea about women's worth. When a man unilaterally decides to give his wife an allowance, he is saying, "I don't trust you to know what you're doing."

The Great Depression of 1929 left a hideous scar on our entire society. Millions of Americans plunged overnight from plenty to poverty, from abundance to scarcity.

Its damage is manifest in major toxic behaviors and beliefs handed down from our parents. Older women who utter such statements as, "There is not enough to go around," "If I spend it, there won't be any more," or "Money is more important than love in any marriage" are echoing the frightened sentiments of an earlier age.

Noted Elaine, 71:

> Nothing stimulates greed quite as much as scarcity, it seems. Whenever there's an economic depression or recession, people gather their material belongings around them just a little tighter. I know I do. And nothing isolated the women in my family more definitively than the lack of mobility, the lack of stylish clothing and the lack of money in general that kept my own mother isolated after the Depression took its toll on our family.

> I remember her complaints after the Depression hit: "We can't afford to look nice." "We can't afford to have our friends over for dinner." "We can't afford to travel." "Our furniture is wearing out, and we can't buy anything new." She cried most of the time. Her belief in looking good was so strong it limited everything about her life. And for us children, too. It wasn't until the Second World War that I was able to get outside of Boston, I was so entrenched in the "can't afford" mode. It still pales me.

To investigate at close range the condition of older women's economic resources and their financial futures is to venture into the very heart of fear. Economic hardship has long been a consequence of divorce, leaving women stranded with children to rear on their own. Recalls Jean, "I raised three daughters in the wealthy suburbs, just on credit cards. I spent most of my time, when I wasn't drinking and working as a private secretary, 'kiting' checks to meet the mortgage and keep my kids satisfied at the mall. Not having money was my biggest secret."

Olivia was financially bereft following her divorce from an attorney with influential political connections. "I've never known an attorney's wife who divorced her hus-

band and didn't get ripped off," she said. "Judges and lawyers take care of each other. It's the old boys' buddy system. They make sure their wives are powerless and pen-
niless." Olivia's husband is a practicing alcoholic. Her Al-
Anon group is comprised entirely of attorneys' ex-wives
who know exactly how she feels.

Many people believe that older women are bitter and
unfeeling. If they are, economic injustice helps to explain
it. The fact is older women who experienced the cataclys-
mic effects of the Great Depression often feel the need to
stay angry and on guard, fearing that if they don't they
will simply fold in the face of sudden economic losses that
often do occur. I know of women who have gone from
$60,000 to $100,000-a-year incomes when their husbands
were alive and productive to living on $9,000 in annual
retirement benefits. Like the Great Depression, from suf-
ficiency to scarcity.

Economic decisions concerning the needs of older wom-
en are made by men in Congress and others responsible
for dispensing Social Security benefits. But what gives
these people the right to determine unilaterally what an
older woman needs? At election time countless promises
are made to attend to the needs of the aging, but in fact
very little has been done to improve their financial situation. In fact benefits have been cut. In my interviewing I
discovered that more than 70 percent of my subjects live
on the poverty line.

In order for older women to make sure that they get
what they need after retirement, or when they are widowed or rendered disabled, they must have a larger voice
in government policymaking. The time has come to gather
together to advocate for change.

Margaret

"After raising five sons, all highly competitive athletes,
I finally realized that their coach father was my higher
power as well as theirs," said Margaret, 64. "How could I
have been any kind of winner in that family, when the

role model was designed to be aggressive and strong? My parents had taught me to be passive. I was angry!

"For years I was their taxi driver. My custom was not to have a drink until school was out at three o'clock. Then, after delivering my sons to their respective track meets, football practice, basketball tournaments, tennis matches, I would go home to drink my Manhattans alone. Always heavy on the bitters, so no one could smell it on my breath, I told myself. It got worse. I became paranoid about my drinking, retired to the pantry and stopped drinking in public at all. Then I stopped *being* in public at all. I became totally isolated and drank alone.

"After the boys had all gone off to college, I continued to drink at home alone and my husband stayed on the athletic scene. In a two-year period he had two affairs with other women, both 20 years younger than us and both physical education teachers. At 57 I had a breakdown, hit my bottom, stopped drinking and learned in treatment how destructive the whole setup was.

"Now I can kick off my heels, let life flow, look at the signs of my success. Today my kids respect me; they don't insult me anymore. That's because I respect myself, and I have told them they cannot have a relationship with me unless they treat me with the respect they have always expected me to show them. They said, 'Show us how to do that, Ma, and we'll do it.' Communication. What a discovery. My life is better now than it has ever been."

How did Margaret do that? "It took two years of sobriety just to convince my family I was serious about not drinking. I had tried to stop drinking at least a dozen times before. But my kids would always find me passed out after the game or stumbling and struggling to 'pass' as sober. After two years of abstinence, with a strict, no-nonsense AA sponsor, I finally could begin to meet commitments and take responsibility for my feelings. My husband refused to attend Al-Anon meetings. He was plenty angry at first when I sobered up. It seemed the more agreeable I became, the nastier and more critical he got. We switched roles. He came home drunk a couple of times and flat-out told me he wanted a separation. One Sunday, after an uncommonly difficult family dinner, during which Fred sniped and snapped at me, I fled from the table in tears. My middle son, Jack, always the arbitrator, followed me into the kitchen, put his arms around me and suggested that we seek couple counseling.

"I was dreadfully frightened at such an idea, for I had heard often that most couples divorced when the alcoholic got sober. And I was scared Fred would refuse to go to counseling. But my AA sponsor knew of a priest in Philadelphia, a hundred miles away, who was a certified addictions counselor. I still believe it was the cleric collar that first got Fred there. Well, we drove there in silence every Wednesday afternoon, and it began to work. One day after the counselor learned we couldn't talk to each other about our feelings, or just about anything for that matter, without fighting, he instructed Fred to pretend I was sitting in this empty chair and to talk to me.

"Fred ended up crying and screaming that his greatest fear was that I was going to get drunk again. And then he said the strangest thing. He said he wished I would. At least he'd know how to act, he said. Then it came out that he wanted to retire but was terrified to be around me very much because he was afraid he'd say or do something that would set me off. And then he was crying really hard and saying that he was most afraid I was going to die like his mother had died of alcoholism. And he also slipped in there that he was afraid I was smarter than he was. I hadn't known it, but he said his life was miserable from the day I stopped drinking!

"I was afraid we'd lose everything we had then, but we followed all our counselor's suggestions. After several weeks, though, I realized that Fred was eager for the counseling, that he was the one who made sure we were there on time. (We used to be notoriously late for every appointment, whether it was social or business.) Then one day on our way to the counselor we talked in the car about how we had all our life together communicated with a third person present, and that happened when our kids were present, too, and that we really had filtered our desires and our feelings and our decisions through our children.

"I remember I was driving and that we were stopped at a red light, when Fred said, 'Peg, do you realize that we're sitting here, right now, on our way to see a counselor to learn to communicate, that we *are* communicating, just the two of us? I don't see anybody else here. Do you?' We laughed, and Fred reached over and squeezed my hand, and we looked right at each other. I felt so close to him that day. We kept going to that counselor for over two years and following his suggestions. It wasn't always easy either.

"One directive the counselor gave us that I believe to be the most helpful in dealing with our anger with each other was that we talk every morning about what each of us needed to hear and to say that day. Just for that day. And we weren't allowed to say the same thing two days in a row. We weren't allowed to save it up. It was very hard at first because neither of us trusted the other to accept what we wanted to hear. We fell into the old pattern of defending our own past behaviors. We were also not allowed to use the words no, never and not. It turned out to be extremely positive and reassuring for both of us.

"That was six years ago and we're still doing it. We read the third-step prayer together every morning, too. I'm still sober and Fred is retired. He coaches a co-educational high school basketball team, the first in our community. We attend open Sunday morning AA breakfasts together, but he still doesn't attend Al-Anon, and I don't push it. I believe the best thing about our lives is that we talk to each other and listen to each other. We don't talk about my alcoholism or my recovery very much, but Fred honors my disease and respects my program and he doesn't drink now at all. We have two grandchildren. I absolutely love being a grandmother. Two of our sons are in AA. The other son doesn't drink, but his wife does. It's amazing. She even *looks* like me."

CHAPTER SIX

Mothers And Daughters

Tomes have been written about the intricacies of relationships between mothers and daughters. While not the focus of this book, some key issues regarding mothers and daughters in recovery demand observation. In no other area of human relationships does the need for healing from the effects of generational hand-me-down toxicity become more evident than in the relationships between mothers and daughters. It is within the context of this relationship that we are able to see increasing numbers of both older and younger women becoming motivated to change.

I love to see mothers and their adult daughters together in the same room. Mercifully this scene is becoming more and more familiar to therapists across the country. As the formal therapeutic process begins, one can see between them great love that is inexpressible. A powerful connection is present as they regard each other tentatively across the room, longing to take a risk but fearing conflict, not wanting to appear rude or angry or cruel. To risk confrontation, they believe, is to risk losing each other. By the time a mother reaches my doorstep she is afraid that she may have already lost her daughter, that her daughter has already abandoned her. She is often overly concerned about what her daughter thinks and feels about her, and she is intent upon defending her parenting methods of years gone by. At the close of their initial session a mother will often express a feeling of concern for her daughter. "I really want you to grow and be happy," she may say to her daughter. Implicit in this, however, is the additional message, "But I don't want you to change," for she fears that her daughter will grow away from her.

These mothers and daughters return and attentively hang on to each other's words in subsequent sessions. It is an eye-opener for the therapist to observe how these women are in "different movies." They have shared the daughter's lifetime of years and have numerous experiences in common, yet their realities are vastly dissimilar. Eager to learn about each other's convictions, they seem genuinely surprised to discover that they have such divergent perceptions about what has passed between them. "I didn't know you felt that way!" one of them may exclaim. "I always thought that . . ." It is delightful to observe them beginning to see eye-to-eye, open and level and daring to risk being vulnerable with each other, sharing their hopes and fears. Little by little they become more honest and direct. They also become more assertive, each learning to get her needs met without hurting the other. This is truly a wonderful process.

A Mother's Work Is Finally Done

Essential to this mutual recovery process is the acknowledgment by both mother and daughter that the mother's job of parenting is finished. Without this recognition there will not develop between them the kind of equanimity that will enable them to listen to and learn from each other. Many older women will not listen to younger women, holding to the idea that they as the elder know best.

But our learning never stops. Whatever our age, we need to remain open to expanding our knowledge. If we close ourselves off simply because of chronological age differences, we are limiting ourselves. The recovering older woman needs to open herself to learning from her daughter, this younger person of her own flesh to whom she has given birth and reared. She must see her as an autonomous individual who possesses experience and knowledge and the practiced faculties of reasoning and logic. The daughter, on the other hand, must recognize, as arduous as it may be, that this mother who reared her is no longer an authority figure to whom she must defer or rebel against, but is someone who is learning to become a friend. In these new roles the mother and daughter can now acquire mutual respect.

Many older women, unfortunately, do not recognize that their parenting days are over. They go on being overly involved in their grown children's business. This involvement, without solicitation from their children, renders them caretakingly co-dependent.

Some of the following questions may help you determine whether or not you are being co-dependent with your adult children:

- Do you go through your children's mail, dresser drawers or closets?
- Do you ask them how much they pay for their belongings (car, clothes, etc.)?
- Do you give them unsought advice regarding schools, careers, vacations or investments?
- Do you worry about their welfare when they are not in daily or weekly contact with you?
- Do you become angry and jealous when you learn that your children consult each other in their decision-making and try to keep it a secret from you?

- Do you constantly worry that your daughter or son may be telling a therapist terrible things about you?
- Do you frequently rearrange your children's hair, collars, buttons, pick lint from their clothing, adjust their shoulder pads?
- Do you ever rearrange the furniture in your children's home without their consent?
- Do you feel lonely and abandoned when you learn that your children have got together socially and not invited you to join them?
- Do your children make jokes about your need to be the "switchboard operator," the "family publisher," the "Queen Bee" or "Dr. Mom?"
- Do you still supervise your adult children's cooking, marketing and budgeting?
- Do you frequently criticize your children's parenting techniques?
- Do you often compare and contrast one child's characteristics and behaviors with another's?
- Are you concerned that your children will spend foolishly what you bequeath them in your will?

Fear Of Failure

For many older women a primary obstacle to recovery from co-dependence is their deep-seated fear of facing their failures as parents. These women are afraid to say simply, "Perhaps I did something wrong," dreading the ensuing guilt and shame. The co-dependent woman, being an all-or-nothing thinker, believes that she has two choices only: either she must firmly defend all of her methods of mothering as having been absolutely right and correct or she must blame herself totally, saying, "I did it *all* wrong. I'm a bad person, a bad mother, a bad woman, *mea culpa*. Nobody loves me so I might as well die right now."

Many mothers have indeed suffered painful and confusing criticism from their children:

Says Irene, 58:

> My oldest daughter is furious with me because *she didn't get to go to boarding school.* My youngest daughter is furious with me because *I sent her to boarding school.*

Sexism plays a role in this as well: many women have sons who refer not only to their mothers but to all women as inferior to themselves. The accusations by sons and daughters go on and on like an endless chant: "She did it wrong. Mom did it wrong." Fathers, whose traditional role demands little involvement in the parenting process, in most cases manage to sidestep censure. Says 61-year-old Karen, whose spouse was alcoholic and unemployed while their children were growing up:

> It's so much easier to blame the parent who was there. I was there. You're darned right I was there, going crazy, raising six kids alone with a high school education and not one bit of help. And so stuck in the absurd pride and shame that I learned from my own mother that I took a bus to a neighboring town to buy groceries so my neighbors and friends wouldn't know I was forced to use food stamps. Now, that is insanity. But I was there.

Admission Of Failure

A question I asked women in my interviews was, "What has been most difficult for you in your recovery from co-dependence?" More than half of them said that most grievous was to recognize the harm that they passed on to their own children. Said Theresa, 67, in recovery for three years:

> I had to face that my message to Linda was, "Take my feelings, absorb my pain for me, but don't express them. You know that I cannot stand your pain and anger, so keep my feelings to yourself. When you cry, I will tell you that you are too soft, too overemotional, too sensitive. I will tell you that you cannot do hard things. And you cannot possibly be happy because I am so sad." That was the toughest realization that I had. That I abused my daughter

by not allowing her her own feelings and handing mine to
her to deal with and fix.

Said Elaine, a physical therapist in her late 50s:

> My pain is in seeing in my daughter the combined ef-
> fects of her father's and my conversations with each other.
> My daughter is a competent physician, an obstetrician. But
> my own father's message to me and my husband's message
> to my daughter are concentrated in her to form such low
> self-esteem as to cause chronic depression: "You will fail.
> You will be found out. You are stupid." And then there was
> my own father's message to me, as well as my husband's
> message to me, which I internalized and as the unwitting
> negative role model passed on to her: "Yes, I am no good,
> and I will be discovered for the fraud that I am. I am bad
> and imperfect. Yes, I will fail." My pain is in seeing the
> concentration of all these values reflected in my daughter's
> obesity, depression, suicidal tendencies and prescription
> drug addiction.

Admitting one's failures is a painful yet powerful turning point in recovery. Said Gloria:

> I am 59 and have four grown children. Two are addicts.
> I am just now learning the rules and regulations of ap-
> propriate social behavior. It's too late to teach my children
> those rules. My pain is in letting go of their lives. I want
> so badly to go back and redo, reteach them. I cry because
> I learned for myself too late to teach my own children
> how to hold a fork. I can only teach them by staying
> sober myself.

It may be reassuring to know that despite a mother's
failures, her children possess a well of love for her. Again
and again I have witnessed this in my work with mothers
and daughters. Not that mothers are instantly forgiven;
to do so would be premature and counterproductive. But
in taking the truth to a level of shared consciousness, in
getting mothers and daughters out of separate movies
and to stardom in the same one, finally they can communicate, and hope springs forth. Says Harriet, 56, "It's taken

me a lot of years of my life to say to my daughter, 'I want you in my life and I love you,' and I'm damned if I'm going to give that up."

Dysfunction, Past And Present

A complicating factor for the older woman with children is that she is faced with recovering not from just one dysfunctional role but from two: from her own history as an abused or neglected child in an alcoholic or otherwise dysfunctional family and from her role as mother of her own unwell family. As some of the members of my older women's groups have said, "I feel torn. I have daughters and sons, but I am also the daughter of a sick family system. How am I to act and react?"

An older woman in recovery must first address her issues as the child of a dysfunctional home. This is the initial and primary perspective. In this way she will develop a comprehensive understanding of her life and the part she was cast to play, however unconscious, during her child-hood drama. From this she will begin to see how she, in turn, handed predictably damaging roles to her children to play in the family she was forming. She will come to see the purpose these roles played in maintaining the imperfect balance of her dysfunctional families, past and present.

Marjorie, in her 60s, was one of five siblings. Her parents were both alcoholic. As far as they were concerned only her older sister could do everything right. For her part:

> I always screwed up. I couldn't keep promises, I felt terrible about myself and never lived up to anyone's stan-dards. I was dreadfully sorrowful without knowing why. Mom was so busy drinking with Dad she didn't have time to understand what was going on. She cried a lot when we were kids. She kept saying through her tears, "Why don't you girls try to get along. Just once. Be nice. Please be nice." When Dad died from an alcohol-related disease when I was 30, although I had been away from home for 13 years, I felt I had caused his death. If only I had been a more obedient child, if only I had tried harder to be a good

student, if only I had listened to him, maybe he would have
lived long enough to forgive me and we could have been
friends. I grieved longer and harder than anyone in the
family. I even intentionally overdosed on tranquilizers. No
one could understand. I was the one he was meanest to,
the one he hit the hardest. Yet I loved him dearly and
wanted more than anything to please him. I carried this
grief well into my own aging years.

She now realizes that she carried these unresolved
issues into her own family:

I have three children. They were all taught that their
grandfather was kind, smart and very much the hero.
They knew nothing of the battlefield that was my childhood. I glorified my father and made him a hero. Not only
to my children, but in my own mind, I considered him to
be a true martyr. Now I know he was a victim who
needed victims.

It was only after Marjorie began to recover from her
dual addictions to alcohol and Valium that she began to
address her co-dependence, finally comprehending how
her family's roles and pathology worked in concert to feed
her pain throughout most of her life.

Sometimes simple rites of passage that members of a
family go through generation after generation unearth
pockets of pain. Edith, 56 and divorced, describes one
such situation:

I know we are a sick family, but I've got my own pain
now with one of my daughters getting married. With every wedding in my family now, I go through some of my
own pain. I have two issues: the loss of my daughter and
the loss of my own dream that I had when I was married.
And then the question arises, will what happened to me
happen to her?

To help distinguish one role from the other, older wom-
en may wish to read books on recovery twice, the first
time from the perspective of the child, the second as the
mother. For example, in reading a book on issues of chil-

dren of alcoholic families, first she will do so as the aching child in such a family, and then as an adult who perpetuated that behavior in her own family. This way of reading will bring back memories of each role, adding to her storehouse of knowledge and experience and enhancing her recovery.

I Don't Want To Be Like My Mother

"Who are you?" I will often ask a new client. "What is your identity? How do you perceive yourself?"

"Well, I don't know," many will respond, "but I do know that I don't want to be like my mother."

Marilyn, 61, and her 31-year-old daughter, Victoria, came to see me together. Marilyn is a recovering alcoholic with seven years of sobriety. Victoria is a single career woman. When the two came into my office for our first session, they brought with them a cloud of rage toward each other. Both were tight-lipped, silent, slant-eyed and blaming. The conversation was sprinkled with "you always," "you never" and "I'd just once like to see you do so-and-so."

It was apparent that both mother and daughter were seeking validation from the other. "I don't know how you got your low self-esteem," said the mother. "I tell you every day that I love you."

"But you never tell me that I'm worthwhile," Victoria retorted. She repeated this again and again in that first session until the words became a kind of mantra for her.

All too soon it became obvious to me why Marilyn told her daughter every day that she loved her: Her own mother had never told her that she loved her. Marilyn, therefore, tried to make up for the pain that her mother had caused her and told her own daughter again and again and again how much she loved her. She did not, however, demonstrate to Victoria's satisfaction that she actually thought her worthy of her love. Marilyn's words and her behavior were not congruent. She lacked authenticity. As Victoria pointed out, "I love you" was often followed with, "But you don't have good taste in clothing," or "I hate the way you wear your hair," or "It's too bad that your grades aren't as good as your brother's."

It also unfolded that Victoria telephoned her mother every day from home to report her comings and goings and to seek her counsel. And Marilyn called her own mother, who was 82 and ill, also to seek her support and to hear what she had not heard in 61 years — the words "I love you." Victoria does not want to be like her mother, and Marilyn does not want to be like her mother, yet both of these women crave their mother's love and approval.

Most daughters love their mothers even in the worst of dysfunction. When a daughter says she does not want to be like her mother, she may be saying that she does not want to adopt her mother's belief system and behavior. She may be saying that she does not want to be angry and abusive like her mother. She may be saying that she does not want to react to her father's anger the way she saw her mother react and that she does not want to repeat this behavior with her own husband. She may be saying that she does not want to be overcontrolling or oversubmissive. Or perhaps she is saying that she does not want to be emotionally withdrawn and paralyzed. In effect when a daughter says she doesn't want to be like her mother, she is saying that she does not want to be co-dependent.

Most younger women are not aware that what they see in their mothers are unresolved conflicts, unaddressed issues. A generation ago, a good woman was a stepped-on doormat and kept anger under wraps, not complaining about any kind of pain.

Many a younger woman has a common wish for her caretaker mother: "I wish you would decide to live your life for yourself and to reclaim your life for yourself," she says. "All of your life you have been living for someone else. But *I* cannot and will not do that." She goes on to say, "I want to feel my feelings. I want to make my own choices. I want to be treated equally. I do not want to be a doormat. I want to develop according to how I want to be." She has never seen her mother do these things and so has disdainfully turned her back on her. She is not aware that her mother did not do these things simply because society did not allow her to do so.

At the base of it the young woman who says she does not want to be like her mother is saying that she did not and still does not have the kind of role model she needs. Older women must hear this message from their daughters and begin to model a new way — a way that is actually an old way. They may consider returning to the classic characteristics of the traditional older woman. This is not a white-haired old lady in that apron and with that hot apple pie, but she is the older woman who knows how to listen attentively, who speaks wisely and who has opinions of her own. This older woman affirms and validates her younger protegee. Instead of telling her daughter, "Do this! Do that!" she waits respectfully, ready to offer her assistance if asked. To assume this new role is to stop caretaking and to start a friendship. In this way she can hope to make a contribution to her daughter's life, and perhaps in the process give her a more positive image of a person she may wish to resemble.

Common Issues

In my work with mothers and daughters a number of issues commonly emerge:

Nuance Dysfunction

This is a term that I have coined, frequently having observed this dynamic as particularly common to mothers and daughters. *Nuance dysfunction* is a subtle mode of communication used by one person for the purpose of punishing or pushing another person away. Mothers and daughters take turns using it with each other.

Nuance dysfunction has to do with believing that another person ought to be able to recognize and satisfy another person's need without that person saying a word about it. The consequence of this nuance behavior is a sense of disappointment when the person fails to intuit properly and respond as expected.

Many a mother believes that, "My daughter should know me well enough to guess what's going on with me without my actually having to tell her." Many daughters have the same belief about their mothers. "I thought you knew that I wouldn't be there by 4:00. I'm always late," says a daughter when she meets her mother at a movie theater a half-hour late. "You know me well enough never to call me on Wednesdays," fumes a mother upon being interrupted during a business meeting by her daughter's innocent and infrequent phone call.

A perfect example of nuance dysfunction was manifested in a series of exchanges regarding Christmas presents between a mother and daughter, Jeannine and Jodie, who are my clients. Their tradition was to give each other wearing apparel as gifts. "What do you want for Christmas?" Jodie asked. Jeannine replied, somewhat hurt, "Well, you know what I like." Jodie was expected to know what Jeannine wanted without having to be told. Indeed, with practice many daughters do know their mothers' preferences. If they do not know, however, they are hesitant to ask, for fear that their mothers will view them as uncaring or insensitive.

Jodie experienced confusion and growing resentment. She felt herself to be trapped, a painfully familiar feeling. Forced to guess, Jodie selected a khaki sweater as her mother's Christmas present. She doesn't feel joy or satisfaction with her purchase, but exhaustion, anxiety and uncertainty. Sure enough, her worst fears are realized when Jeannine opens the gift and tells her, "But this isn't the khaki that's popular this year!" Jodie's sin lies in not having intuited the precise shade of khaki her mother preferred. No matter what her choice, Jodie was set up to feel wrong, less than perfect.

The nuance continues: Jeannine asked her daughter, "What do you want for Christmas?" Jodie answered, "I'll take whatever you give me. I love you and whatever you get me is just fine." Following this exchange, Jeannine

decided to give Jodie a check for the amount of money that
she normally would have spent on some sort of wearing
apparel. The next thing I knew Jodie was in her therapy
session complaining that her mother didn't care enough
about her to pick out a Christmas gift anymore.

Ultimately, nuance dysfunction is a form of manipulation between people who are ostensibly intimate to blame,
to control and to find each other wanting.

In recovery we must stop expecting others to read our
minds and stop punishing them when they cannot. We
move beyond nuance dysfunction by being clear and specific
in our verbal communications about what we want and
need. This is our responsibility and we need to accept it.

Mom's Favoritism/Scapegoating

As a mother recovers from her caretaker role, she will
need to address an issue that recurs in dysfunctional families: the favoritism she has shown to certain of her children and the deleterious ways she treated others. She
needs to prepare to face courageously her daughters and
sons as they confront her on this issue, as well they may.

Favoritism is inevitable in any dysfunctional system. A
co-dependent mother will, for example, commonly show
favoritism to the hero of the family, the well-behaved child
who obeys all the rules, helps her out and does well in
school. This child, although enjoying having been chosen
as Mom's favorite, also is vulnerable to the slings and ar-
rows of his siblings' jealousy. The child who is the scape-
goat, on the other hand, who is risk-taking, impulsive and
forever in trouble in order to gain attention, will certainly
be anything but his mother's favorite. As the family's disease progresses, the manipulating caretaker tends unknow-
ingly to generate divisiveness and competition among her
children and even her grandchildren, all to keep balance in
the household, however painful it becomes.

Emotional walls between a mother and her children
often hark back to her unresolved issues. Andrea, 59, in
recovery from alcoholism, understood her long-standing

problems with her eldest son, Ted, only after she began to recover from co-dependence. Her husband, who had been an active alcoholic, died when she was in her 30s. After his death, she found it terribly painful to look at the face of her son as he grew older and more closely resembled her husband.

Andrea believed that she should not be angry at her dead husband, but indeed she was. This anger she unconsciously transferred to Ted, for whom she found it impossible to have positive feelings. She blamed him unmercifully. She labeled him, calling him lazy and unkempt. She alienated her son's affections. I worked with both of them in therapy. In recovery she finally realized what she had done. After facing her truth head-on, Andrea was able to make amends to Ted. Happily their relationship has improved in ways precious and valuable to them both.

It is essential to her own recovery and to her relationships with her children that a mother honestly face her practices of favoritism and scapegoating. She must be prepared when her children begin to confront her with such questions as, "I always thought you loved my brother best," or "I always thought that you favored my sister, is it true?" What is important is that she not blame herself but that she validate her child's reality. She must make an effort to understand and explain her behavior. It is not enough just to say, "Well, I was sick then and that's why I did it." She must practice discernment in order to understand the circumstances that contributed to her behavior as her child describes it. She needs to be able to say, honestly and compassionately, "Yes, I can understand why you feel that way, and you have every right to those feelings."

Revealing Secrets

Many older women keep from their children something they consider a terrible secret: the truth about their own dysfunctional childhoods. Fay, 72, spoke for many of the women I interviewed when she told me:

I suffered so much when I was a young woman, a young
mother. I suffered a lot from my own family of origin and
their sickness, and I did not want my daughters and sons
to have those same problems. I didn't want to let them
know that I was in deep pain.

Not only had many of the older women I interviewed
been born into alcoholic families and later married alcoholics, but many were themselves in recovery from alcoholism. Yet they chose not to tell their children about this
family heritage, attempting at nearly any cost to keep
their pain a secret and hence, presumably, protect their
children. But this never works. Most children at an early
age are remarkably adept at perceiving their parents' pain,
although they do not fully comprehend it and generally
believe that they caused it. Ultimately the mother who
keeps secrets is depriving her children of valuable information and so inadvertently drives an emotional wedge
between herself and her family.

"You didn't have it so bad," my client Louise told her
mother, Marie, during our therapy session. "You've had
everything you wanted all your life." At this point Marie
finally revealed that she had suffered from alcoholism
during most of her daughter's childhood. As surprising
and disturbing as this revelation was, it enabled Louise to
turn a corner with her mother. At last Louise was able to
demystify many confounding aspects of her relationship
with her mother. She began to feel compassion for her
mother. Where there had once been resentment, now
came acceptance.

It is crucial that we share the truth with our children,
including a full recounting of our disease. Not only does
this promote recovery and healthy relationships with our
children, but this is the way we can begin to avoid what
is termed the "generational skip phenomenon" common to
many dysfunctional families. In this, one generation of a
family suffers from alcoholism, for example, while the
next generation, thoroughly ashamed and determined not
to allow this to happen to them, fervently avoids any

allusion to it with their own offspring. This third generation, totally oblivious to familial and genetic tendencies, is left floundering in ignorance of their own vulnerability to alcoholism.

This is important information. For the recovering mother, sharing her secrets with her children — weaving together recovery, personal history and family history — is a responsible and loving act.

Sexual Abuse: Validating Your Daughter's Truth

Many daughters of toxic families have been victims of sexual abuse by their parents, other relatives or other persons known to the family. As painful as it may be, mothers of these daughters need to acknowledge this truth. Perhaps they denied it in the past. Perhaps they closed their eyes to it while it was occurring. Perhaps they had no inkling about it. But we must remember that providing a protected and safe environment for our children is the primary responsibility of parenting.

In recovery the truth about sexual abuse must emerge and be faced. The daughter who comes to her mother reporting that she was sexually abused as a child, most of all needs to be believed. In some cases, a mother must look long and hard at the denial and possibility of repression that fed her disease. She must become aware of her tendency to self-delude. A mother who herself abused her children must realize that she may not have immediate recall of certain events and may have even rewritten her child's history entirely.

"We tried our best to be good parents," a deluded mother, presenting her own spin on her complaining daughter's story, may say. "We gave you everything you wanted. You didn't have a bad time. And I did, after all, have a lock put on your bedroom door, so nothing could have happened to you."

As recovering women we must recognize that we repressed our painful feelings and so sometimes have no immediate recall of what actually occurred. Once a mother acknowledges her denial, she can begin to forgive herself and open up to her child's reality.

If you are the mother of an adult daughter (or in some cases, a son) who shares with you that sexual abuse has occurred, the following may prove helpful to both of you in your response:

- First and foremost it is important to recognize that your child's act of confronting what may be your family's darkest secret is a courageous act. Honor her courage and you earn her trust. Remember that what happens at this juncture may affect your child's health and happiness for the rest of her life. Recognize that her confrontation is neither an impulsive nor manipulative gesture, but that she has most likely thought it out and planned it very carefully, often with the help of a recovery counselor.

- If you find yourself wondering why your daughter never told you about this before, keep in mind that her own denial system may have been operative. It is possible that your daughter "forgot" for many years her father's sexual abuse in order to convince herself that she had the good father she wanted.

- Try to provide a setting for your pre-arranged discussion that is positive and conducive to trust and open communication. A neutral space is preferable, such as a peaceful park or a private place comfortable for both of you but away from your own individual "turfs."

- Keep in mind that your daughter is a rational adult and deserves the respect of being heard. Listen to *all* of what she has to say before you respond. Actively seek to determine what she needs. Her immediate need may be that you simply hear her. Under no circumstances do you alter her reality by interrupting or correcting what she says. It is essential to her well-being and process that you wait for her to finish and to request your response.

- Write down details and take a few minutes to collect your thoughts and memories before you make your response.
- When you are ready to respond, paraphrase in detail what you have just heard your daughter say to you. Be specific. Not only does this assure that you understand her, but in being specific you are more likely to find clarity yourself.
- Communicate honestly what you remember about the events she has described. Perhaps your own denial has made recall difficult; however, if you believe that what your daughter remembers could actually have occurred, say so.
- Remember that change does not usually happen instantly, but results through persistence, patience and purposefulness. This initial encounter places you in the ground-shifting position of rebuilding your relationship with your daughter.
- Relax. The entire problem does not have to be solved right now. What is important is to establish trust. Once this is accomplished, communication between you will continue despite the fear you may have that life itself is contingent upon what is said in the next sentence.
- If you have not done so already, the greatest gift you can give your daughter now is to seek treatment for co-dependence. If, for whatever reason, you choose not to do this while knowing that what she is telling you is the truth, your next best gift is the validation of her reality and, if you can possibly do it, a sincere apology.
- You were there in that place with your daughter. Now tell her you are ready to stand by her. Make a declaration of your own conscience. Tell her your own truth as you now know it.

Greta is the author of five published science fiction novels, a nationally known speaker, women's rights advocate and a lesbian feminist, age 68. She is a recovering alcoholic and an incest survivor in recovery for 12 years. B.C.D. are the initials of her grandmother's maiden name. She talked about the term, "maiden name":

> Maiden means chaste or virgin, girlish and modest. So no woman's birth name will have real force or great strength in the world until she changes it to the name of a lord and master, as his helpmate. This is cunning and subtly eroding to her birthright, which is yet again the name of a lord and master whose name her mother took, as his helpmate. Yes, times are changing, but when I was young, the choice to retain legally my mother's maiden name was not legally mine. Names are very important to our self-esteem. They have always represented family roots and family value in the community. Some women are proud to have their father's family name. I am not.
>
> I was given the name of a person who was my oppressor, my aggressor. Someone who claimed my body and my spirit when I was five years old. I began to reclaim myself over 20 years ago when I joined AA the first time. Then I drank for several years after that. But I felt I truly reclaimed my native rights the day I had my maiden name changed legally. It was a signal of my renascence. I had few rights, I felt. My mother was not interested at all in hearing my story after I dried out. It took me six years to have my name changed. They didn't want to change my father's last name on my records. But the fight was worth it, and I still think of that struggle as an investment in my identity. I've stayed sober, too, since I was able to define who I am!

CHAPTER SEVEN

Community

Loneliness looms largest among the issues older women face, followed by depression, fear of poverty and fear of physical disintegration. All of these lead to social and emotional segregation, a major cause of suicide among the elderly.

Isolation

Isolation is not the mere matter of being alone. We can feel isolated even while we are among other people, whether we are spending time with our family or living alone among huge, anonymous crowds in a skyscraper city. Being married and living under the same roof with one's partner do not preclude a woman being isolated. Members of families not in recovery from addiction are all isolated from each other. Isolation is the experience of being emotionally and socially cut off or separated from other people. It is often described as a feeling of numbness and a state of being outside looking in. It is the experience of not experiencing.

In our recovery isolation is a deadly and all-too-familiar enemy. Every person who is recovering from chemical dependence or co-dependence encounters isolation as the way they lived during their active addictions. Without exception our addictive disease, be it alcohol or food or work or crisis or caretaking, takes us to a place where, rather than relate in an intimate and vulnerable manner with other people, we much prefer the familiar state of isolation. Ironically even as this isolation leads us into danger and possible death, we feel safe. It is cunning, baffling and powerful.

Isolation is a killer. It is self-imposed social apartheid. Contributing to the older caretaking woman's sick role as a martyr, it gives birth to self-pity and resentment. When a woman begins to say to herself, "They don't know me . . . They don't understand me. I can do it all myself. I don't need anyone," or "After all I've done, now that I'm sick and tired nobody's taking care of me, poor little old me" (the PLOM syndrome, as it is called in AA). We can be sure that this woman is in isolation and on the road to martyrdom.

Isolation also compounds when we begin to draw comparisons and contrasts between ourselves and others. We know that we are isolated when, as we observe others happily involved and productive, we feel inferior, useless, insecure and jealous. We are then unable to feel positively about others and are treading the downward spiral. We lose touch with practical reality, our physical limitations and our changes. Isolation steals our discernment from us. Most dangerous to the recovering person, isolation contributes to the possibility of relapse into our disease.

Recovery experts cite the prevention of isolation as being foremost in the prevention of relapse. In choosing isolation over relating to others we deprive ourselves of nurture and thereby are likely to regress into active addiction. We need to connect with people daily. Spouses need to learn to communicate with each other in kind and loving ways. Every day we need to see or at least call friends, neighbors, colleagues, family and other people dear to us. The benefits to us are twofold: We feel a sense of value and belonging in the world, and we gain great satisfaction in making a contribution to others' lives.

Are you connected with people? I often ask this question of my clients. "Oh sure, I watch TV," they may answer. Or "Of course, I read the newspaper." But this is not real connection. This is passive viewing. It is watching the world go by but not communicating or making a contribution. Reading may have great value, but it is not connecting with others. The older woman in recovery must be committed to continue to grow and learn through others. In order to do so she must resist isolation in every way. She must learn relatedness, which simply means involvement with other living creatures, every day, with friends, pets and even plants.

Creating Community

What is the older woman's community? No hard and fast rules apply. Her community varies according to her needs, in the same way it evolved during her younger years. Her choices, we discover, will depend largely upon her roots. Many women I interviewed have told me, "I was born in the city, and now I need to be with other urbanites. I tried living in the suburbs, but that doesn't work for me. I was born in an apartment, and that's where I like to be, that's where I'm comfortable."

My own rural roots pull me back to the land. This is where I am happiest. Long weekends on my farm in Spring Green, Wisconsin, 190 miles from Chicago, are essential to my well-being. Sometimes I arrive at the farm, feeling exhausted or even despondent because of problems that have arisen in my work during the week. By the following morning everything comes together: I hear the birds singing. I watch the deer, the squirrels, the rabbits. I call out to my hills and wait for the reassuring echo. I walk around in the cool grass in my bare feet. This particular kind of community is a connection, not with people but with Mother Earth. This is my spiritual solace, something I find extremely comforting and fulfilling.

But on the farm I need people, too. A most gratifying time is spent talking with my neighbors and their children, watching these young people learn, change and grow. I may spend my morning in an old tire swing with the five-year-old son of a neighbor, playing and discovering with him, then go to a friend's house and talk about a newspaper article we both had read, then go to the hospital to visit a 75-year-old neighbor who is dying of cancer.

One morning I asked one of my neighbors to leave her children with me while she went off to do some errands. And for that little effort that afternoon I found at my back door a huge bag of tomatoes, cucumbers, squash, green beans, onions, radishes — enough to last me for the summer if they would not perish. A wonderful exchange occurs among us. It has taken me years to reach this spiritual place, to become a part of this community. I do my grocery shopping in Spring Green. I also buy my clothes, cosmetics and household items there, thus investing financially in my own community.

We create our community based on exchange: what we need and what we contribute. I have an elderly neighbor, a widow, who finds her community in her AA meetings every Monday night, her weekly Sunday church service, attending art fairs and classical music concerts and walking to the library, where she carefully selects and orders large-print novels. Weekly she visits her hairdresser, a woman she's known for 30 years. She walks one mile three days a week to chat with her best friend, who is bedridden. She converses with visiting nurses and people who deliver Meals on Wheels for another friend. She attends a senior citizen center some afternoons where she helps recycle cans and bottles, does some weaving and plays pinochle. When she needs help, she makes a call and someone comes. When she is able to help, she offers. This is the kind of community that works for her. This woman has balance in her life. She is a recovering older woman.

During my interviews, I learned of one group of recovering alcoholic women in Texas who met in AA. It happened that the husband of one of the women, Connie, had died and left his hobby, a collection of seven 1950s Volkswagen Bugs, sitting in her backyard. "I thought it was a shame that the cars were unused and getting rusty," said Connie, "so I decided to give one to each of my six sister AA members. One of them, a retired Greyhound bus mechanic, volunteered to teach the rest of us how to maintain our cars. Today we all regularly converge on Saturday mornings to tune up our Bugs' engines, change the oil and so on. And twice a year we dress up in wild outfits and have what we call our VW Prism Parade downtown, having painted our cars in every color. We affectionately call ourselves, The Rainbow Bughaus Girls. Everybody in town loves it. Especially the kids. They'd like it if we had a parade every day."

In another interview I spoke with Lottie, a recovering caretaker and grandmother who told me how she set up in her community a drop-in center for recovering grandmothers. "We paint, we have an improvisational acting group, we perform a dance act for nursing home shut-ins, we have bake sales and give lectures in schools," Lottie proudly announces. "Women come from as far as 50 miles to be a part of our group. We have such great fun together."

As I neared completion of my interviewing, I received a call from a woman in a nursing home whom I had interviewed the previous year. She was laughing as she spoke, telling me about a song they were singing. The words went something like this: "You come to see us in this nursing home, you think we look pretty tired, but late at night when the lights go down, everybody gets inspired. Somebody turns on the radio, someone orders pizza to eat, we rock these wheelchairs 'round the halls and sometimes we start trading teeth." She and her friends call themselves the Sideliners, she says, because they are all in wheelchairs. They laugh together. Each of us can and will find our own unique form of community — and some are more unique than others.

Friends

Says Ruth, 71, sober for 12 years and in co-dependent therapy in Florida for two years:

> I've lived in New York all my life and every winter I go to Miami for four months. My family thinks I go there for the warm climate, but I really go for my warm-hearted friends who are my age. Better to be called a "snowbird" in Florida, than to be called up here only when somebody in my family needs money.

Friends are basic to community. While making friends may sound simple enough, many women, especially older ones, have difficulty doing so. Many older women still suffer from the competitiveness that our culture has traditionally engendered among us, encouraging us to vie for the affections of men. As a group we have learned to be critical of each other. Those of us who have been isolated for many years do not connect easily with people. Making friends is a process that we learn through practice.

Developing friendships, much like assertiveness, is simply a healthy way of getting what we need and want. Often, not knowing how to assert these desires, we end up alienated from potential friends. This matter emerges in my therapy groups when I discover that a client has few or no friends. "Well, I went to dinner with Sandra, but she talks too much," one client may say, "and Rebecca is always complaining." When I inquire as to whether or not my client asked Sandra to allow her to speak or told Rebecca that she is unwilling to listen to her barrage of complaints, thereby shifting the mood of the conversation, my client's response often is "Well, no, I didn't."

The issue at hand is one of feedback — honestly speaking to and hearing each other. Many of us are afraid of feedback, fearing possible conflict and rejection. We consider it a form of criticism and back away from giving or receiving it. We find, however, feedback to be one of the most important and valuable tools of our recovery. We actually grow to be grateful for it. "You sound a little angry," someone may inform us or "You seem impatient." This is useful information. We need to hear it, carefully consider it and change our behavior if we deem it necessary. If it is true that we have been coming across angrily, we may appropriately express our anger directly and move on. If we have been impatient, perhaps we'll take a deep breath and make an effort to slow down. In this way feedback — especially the loving sort we get from friends — proves to be a valuable gift that helps us grow. We can come to love and trust this process.

We need to learn to say, "I want to remain your friend, and to this end I need to tell you that what you've just said is really bothering me. Let's check it out and see what really happened here." In some corners of society candidly telling a friend that she is talking too fast, too loudly or is irritating you with her interruptions is unthinkable and considered rude, if not unconscionable. At the very least, doing so may very well cause your friend to become angry. However, when a friend values you and your perceptions, she will make every effort to hear you, no matter how humbling doing so may be. Neglecting to communicate honestly to our friends what we think and feel or, on the flipside, not having our thoughts and feelings heard by them, leads to one end: resentment. In suppressing our feelings and thoughts we become silent critics, emotionally distanced from each other.

This is not to suggest that every little irritation is cause for major discussion. Here again we apply discernment. If something you find annoying in your relationship with your friend is not so bothersome as to make a great difference, if you can be with your friend and love and cherish her regardless of this annoyance, then it is not a big deal. It is a little deal. Accept it and forget it. But if the annoyance is ongoing and presents obstacles to intimacy, dialogue must ensue. In this way both of you learn from each other and grow together.

The need for conflict resolution, so important between friends, is also a major issue in groups. During my interviews I heard a story about a group of older recovering women who encountered a sensitive issue and through an arduous and painstaking process mutually resolved the conflicts that surrounded it. This group of some 30 women met in Al-Anon in Colorado. After several years of establishing relationships through their weekly meetings, twelve of them decided to split from the core group and form a social circle that would focus on their interest in quilting. Several of the Al-Anon old-timers opposed this move, emphatically insisting that the 12 Steps be kept separate from outside activities. Over a period of months much debate ensued, but the quilters finally opted to pursue their mutual interest. They agreed to begin work together on one quilt, with the understanding that they would not discuss personal problems while in the quilting circle. Instead, they would concentrate on sharing their knowledge of quilting and maintaining positive regard for one another during the designated quilting hours. They met one day a week at nine A.M. Their carefully planned schedule included an Al-Anon meeting and brown-bag or potluck lunch, followed by more quilting until late afternoon.

This arrangement worked very well for several months. The women were all delighted with the results. Recalled Marge, 76, a proud quilter for 30 years: "The quilting experience, and the joy we've had together, working and laughing and loving each other, was the first time some of us had ever known comfort and belonging and contentment."

Not only were they able to continue their spiritual sisterhood in Al-Anon, but now each woman found herself contributing personally to the making of art. They were artists! The quilting day became the social event of the week for many of them. Their first quilt was stunning, and the second even more flawless and beautiful. Then one day someone suggested that they enter a quilt for competition in a local art exhibition. This caused great unrest among some of the women. Many feared the loss of their anonymity, which was precious to their sense of safety.

Among their members was Georgia, 70, a retired lawyer and the spouse of a recovering alcoholic physician. Georgia described herself to me as a "feminist from way back." She was one of several women who talked to me about this situation:

> The fostering of competition among women has historically been the source of isolation for us, since the competition of our strengths has traditionally been for men's favors through our sexual attractiveness and nurturance.

> I believed we were not ready to work together to produce a work of art for competition. My sobriety was my priority, and the joy of doing the quilting, working with my hands and being with my sisters, was all I really wanted. The idea of offering my strivings competitively reminded me of the environment of the workplace which I had just left. Of course, I may have been a bit extreme about it, but those were my personal feelings and needs. I nearly quit right there, so alarmed was I at the possibility of such a move splitting the group and risking the loss of my anonymity. I believed that what we had already achieved was just fine. Why tamper with heaven? As we say in AA, "If it works, why fix it?"

The opposing side — because by now there were two sides — said, in effect, "If it works, let's make it even better." They decided to go ahead and enter the quilt in the competition, though anonymously with initials only, so as to ensure safety. A beautifully crafted giant quilt with an alluring Tree of Life pattern was entered and won second place, no small honor in that huge city. Exuberant, the women wanted even more of the exhilaration of winning.

And then, characteristic of all group processes, a conflict arose:

Irene was one of the pioneers of the core Al-Anon group. Although she was an assiduous learner in many respects, in the quilting group she was a passive beginner and worked slowly. This was due in part to her failing eyesight. Her stitching lacked neatness, and she would often miss a stitch and fail to sew in straight rows. This, of course, would win no quilting bees. The other women, not wanting to hurt her feelings, took turns each week after Irene left and furtively redid her work so that their quilts would meet competition standards. Caught up in the fervor of competition, they failed to see that this was unhealthy co-dependent behavior.

Since Irene was unable to see well enough to drive her own car anymore, her niece drove her to and from the group. One afternoon the niece asked to see her aunt's work. One of the other women in the group, in showing her Irene's poor performance, explained that they were redoing her work but had not told Irene because they didn't want to hurt her feelings. The niece, incensed that her aunt was being deceived and her work discounted, told Irene of the group's deception. Irene was devastated but displayed little emotional response. Instead, feigning illness, she stopped going to the quilting sessions altogether.

Shortly thereafter, the quilting group called a meeting of the entire Al-Anon group, seeking counsel of the core group from which they had split. Should they continue, they pondered, to strive to stitch perfect quilts for the high of winning, at the expense of one of their aging sisters? Or should they accept her imperfection and remain faithful to their original purpose: to enjoy and support each other and learn together. The real challenge of these women's recovery, of their love and commitment to each other, was their decision to do things differently from how they would have done it in prerecovery days.

Today this group still meets. Some stitches are sloppy. No one corrects another woman's work. No longer do they show their quilts in public. They have made so many quilts that every one of their members has a quilt on her own bed; yet they still meet for their quilting-and-Al-Anon meeting once a week — in Irene's home, so that she may use her magnifying lamp to see her stitches.

Support Groups As Personal
And Social Responsibility

Every time a group of women forms or a woman joins a support group, they are participating in the creation of a community of valuable advocates who will become increasingly important to them as they grow older. The group may be related to alcoholism, co-dependency or another situation requiring a major life adjustment, including widowhood, cancer recovery or planning intergenerational living. The help that we offer to each other has the potential to move beyond the individual and personal to the social. In mutual support we become advocates for change in our society.

In the early 1970s, for example, I was part of a small group of women who formed the first rape crisis hotline in Chicago. This small but eminently significant contribution acted as the catalyst for a larger and more active movement that, within two or three years, succeeded in having the antiquated and sexist laws regarding rape changed in the state of Illinois.

All women can make a contribution to their community. This is not to say that one needs to contribute vast financial resources or become a community leader. Although taking the helm in some great social venture is certainly an exciting possibility for many, simple contributions can prove just as valuable and satisfying. Some women wish to contribute but do not know how. Remember that contribution is healthier than competition. In relationships with others ask yourself, "What can I do? What am I good at?" There are always appropriate places to offer your services for networking, to make use of your specific skills, from making a 12-Step call to joining a local chapter of the Gray Panthers. Reach out. Ask.

Living In Community And Financial Realities

As we grow older it becomes increasingly important that we women consider the benefits of pooling our financial resources. In some cases doing so may be necessary just to survive. A report of the Illinois Aging Department released in Chicago at the Tenth Annual National Convention of the Older Women's League of 1990 revealed some stark statistics. Women, it notes, live on the average seven years longer than men. However, we are also more likely than men to suffer debilitating health problems and to live in inadequate housing. Said Gwendolyn S. King, U.S. Commissioner of Social Security, "If we do not do something now, the next generation of elderly women could live in extreme despair."

The report goes on to say that in Illinois by the year 2000 there will be one million women over the age of 65. By 2020, with the greying of the baby-boom generation, the number will reach 1.2 million. Women who outlive their spouses will have to support themselves on a single income, adding to the financial strain of Social Security and pension benefits, which even now are not adequate.

Today, the report continues, about 15 percent of women over the age of 65 live in poverty (34 percent of these are elderly black women), compared to only 8 percent of older men. In 1988 the average annual income for an older woman in Illinois was about 56 percent of the older man's average income, or $7,103 for women compared with $12,471 for men. The basic cause of women's greater poverty, the report goes on, is the link between a woman's work history and her Social Security benefits. Women generally have lower earning power, which is largely due to age and sex discrimination. Women are also more likely to leave paid employment to rear their children and to care for an elderly parent. As a result of this "time off" women often lose benefits from Social Security as well as private pension plans.

This sorry state of affairs provides all the more reason for older women to go into recovery, in order to cope in as healthy a manner as possible with what will indeed be a trying situation. It is also important to consider the possibility of networking, pooling our resources, perhaps even developing co-operative living arrangements.

One type of networking that many women, myself included, utilize is the practice of bartering. You do this for me, the system goes, and in return I will do something for you, and no cash will pass between us. For example, I have as a client an older woman who sees me for group therapy every Wednesday and who comes again on Thursday to clean my office. This is our fair trade of services. For older people living on fixed or limited incomes, being able to barter is essential.

Another example of bartering is my 73-year-old friend Bertha, who is retired and lives on a fixed income. One of her favorite activities is volunteering as a guide at the Art Institute of Chicago. A couple of her more affluent friends occasionally give her clothing and other items. As a gesture of gratitude Bertha invites them to the Art Institute. One of her friends is in a wheelchair, the other is on foot, and they become Bertha's personal charges as she escorts them on an enlightening private tour. This is her exchange, her way of paying them back for what they give to her. Not only does barter balance our accounts, but it gives us a sense of usefulness, a feeling of being productive by offering our unique gifts to another.

My friend Bonnie is 66. She barters frequently with a single young woman who lives in the apartment directly above her. The young woman cleans Bonnie's venetian blinds, climbing on a stepladder, something that Bonnie can no longer do comfortably. Bonnie barters with her marvelous steaming chicken soup and kugel, which she has ready on wintry nights when her neighbor comes home, cold and tired, from her office. They have come to share in other ways as well. "I'm so happy I have learned through my 12-Step meetings how to share without being afraid I'm overbearing," said Bonnie. "And I am pleased to learn that at least one young person in this city likes one older person."

Telling Our Stories

A final note on the subject of community: It is important that as older people we share our life stories. This is a powerful way to prevent a sense of isolation, to place our personal journey in the context of the larger community. This is an important gift to women's lore. We may perhaps write on paper or record on tape the details of our lives with as much accuracy as possible. As we do so long-forgotten vignettes pop up in our memories, often delightful and treasurable. This palpable re-creation of our history tells others what happened to us, how we lived, how we have changed, our hopes then and now and how we continue to live day by day. All of this helps to give us a sense that our lives are somehow permanently recorded. This is important, not only to us as individuals, but to our families, our community and society as a whole. We bring to the end of our lives all that has come before us, to teach generations to follow.

In researching this book I visited many institutions: nursing homes; units built to accommodate senior citizens in apartments and cooperative housing units. Several of these offered community services within their specific institutions. Of these a few boasted of making available to the residents weekly therapy groups, drama groups in which the residents could come together in a circle to experientially re-create portions of their lives. These group sessions have proven to be a great boon to the residents' interest in their own longevity, I was told. Their personal life dramas are animated events. The elderly residents stand up, wave their hands, kick their feet, laugh. They also write and talk about their various experiences as if they were still children. The wonder of this is the recognition that the beauty of life need never be lost, even in the controlled environment of a nursing home in which people are so often led to believe that their lives are finished. These residents find here, together, the excitement and joy of the golden years. It is here that they remember their stories and share with others these most personal and precious times. "We understand each other," one older man told me. Here, the sense of community is crucial. "What do you like best?" I asked nursing home residents. Their answer: "Meals, church, drama groups — whenever we are together."

Many years after my sobriety gained hold and the wound of my early child abuse was finally addressed, as memories came sifting back I was delighted to discover many beautifully preserved souvenirs among my own recollections. Some of these remembrances, blocked out completely for many years, have given me great joy and a sense of family tradition, of having roots. I use them now in my older years as gentle caresses in an otherwise largely harsh cache of childhood pain.

Sometimes in the autumn I can hear the sounds of the voices of my mother and her two sisters as they laughed and sang in melodious harmony around a great fire in our backyard on our farm in western Illinois near the Mississippi River, where I was born. Raising apples and peaches for profit was one of my father's avocations.

One picture, that of the migrant pickers and sorters who came annually in the fall and who slept on the top floor in our great house for a few brief weeks, is still enchanting to me. The entire process awakens my visual and olfactory senses as I recall the installation of the conveyor belts in my beloved east barn, converted temporarily each year from its customary dairy purposes to house a bustling miniature commercial plant for packing apples for shipment. I remember the year I had grown just tall enough so that my nose came right up to the edge of the belts. My younger sister was still too short, but I could see and smell it all, the rolling, tilting motion and the savory fragrance of the red Jonathans and the yellow Grimes golden apples as they scooted along the belts. Rows of women stood on each side of these belts, sorting out and discarding wormy apples. The sight of their pink fingers poking through brown cotton gloves, cut at the fingertips to allow dexterity, is forever stored in my visual stash.

One autumn, when I was about five years old, the three women, my mother and my two aunts, decided to make and preserve apple butter. They obtained a giant black pot (which I know now to be like the cauldron that the three witches in Macbeth used), and three wooden spoons, each longer than I was tall. Every morning my aunts would drive to our farm from their respective family homes and the trio would begin working on their project. In my sketchy memory I can go back to the woodpile where I sat chewing bubble gum, watching and listening to those women singing as they stirred, stopping to taste every now and then, wiping their chins on their huge printed aprons. I can still smell the stick cinnamon and the fall woodfire. I hear again those self-designed culinary sorceresses chant and giggle, and I see them once more swaying and bending rhythmically as in tribal dance while they stirred and sang, their breath forming little fogs of moisture around those beautiful faces that I loved.

"Oo-oh, come, come, come, come, come to the church in the wildwood," they sang, seeking affirmation in each other's eyes as their voices met and blended. "Oh, come to the church in the vale." And sometimes if I insisted, they would sing in ancient Hibernian tones, "Oh, Danny Boy, the pipes are ringing . . . "

They "canned" the apple butter, dark and rich, in aluminum gallon pails and sealed each bucket with hot red sealing wax. They must have loved it, for I remember when they reached number seventy-five, they consulted to determine whether or not to "go for a hundred." They did. And then they divided it up. Each one took home thirty-three gallons of apple butter. One of our family's traditional jokes for years was around apple butter. One hundred gallons of it!

CHAPTER EIGHT

The Coming Years

Self-Esteem

Said Josie:

My husband and I are both over 55. He's like a bump on a log . . . He just sits and drinks all day. We used to have two homes. Now we rent a one-bedroom in a third-floor walk-up. We have no retirement, no savings, no health or life insurance. I shall spend the rest of my life working in a semiskilled job just to pay the bills. We can never take vacations or go to the opera. My stereo is broken — I can't even listen to opera. We can't even afford to pay for our daughter's wedding dress. I feel powerless.

Josie explained in our interview that she remained in her marriage with her alcoholic husband by reason of the "in sickness and in health, 'til death do us part" promise in her marriage vows. Was there ever written a marriage vow that was intended even to suggest that one must forfeit one's own spirit in the face of chronic abuse?

The term "self-esteem" has been defined as one's reputation with oneself. Self-esteem is the antonym of other-esteem or external reference. Having self-esteem, or being self-referenting, is believing and behaving according to the values, opinions and goals of one's self. This can be frighteningly foreign to older women in widowhood, divorce and early recovery from chemical or co-dependence. We are accustomed to hearing the term, "low self-esteem" far more frequently than we hear "high self-esteem," simply because the former is more broadly applicable to the majority of women in our culture.

Before we can characterize ourselves as having a high level of self-esteem, such contributing qualities as self-confidence, assertiveness, self-respect, independence, autonomy, dignity and self-love need to be evident in our lives. In turn, to survive, these qualities need an environment of safety and trustworthiness. Here is a key to maintaining our self-esteem as we age. In the last decade, with the federal government's vast reduction of allocations for social services for the elderly, thousands of older citizens are no longer safe or adequately cared for. So where is the safety and trustworthiness of our people?

Every woman needs an advocate, someone who will speak for her, who will exert power to ensure her physical safety and the safety of her self-esteem during those times she cannot act for herself. This does not mean that the advocate actually gives the care needed; it means that the advocate sees to it that quality care is provided on an ongoing basis, when and how and where that becomes necessary. An advocate is not the same as executor of your estate; nor does an advocate necessarily have power of attorney, although you may wish to consider that as well. It is the responsibility of each older woman reading this book to begin to make the choice of an advocate for herself now, while she is able.

Don't wait for someone to come forward to volunteer. Choose someone you trust, who will likely outlive you, who truly believes in equal rights for all, perhaps a feminist, male or female, who is dependable, who is honest and who is willing to give time and energy to *your* welfare. Essentially, this person will become your own personal social worker.

First, be sure to talk with that person. *Ask* the person. Do not simply *name* the person in the presumption that she or he will be comfortable with assuming the duties and obligations accompanying such a request. If you do not know someone whom you can trust enough to become your advocate, then it is time to examine your ability to be intimate. Look around in your 12-Step groups. Get to know a younger person. Stretch. Take a risk. What a precious opportunity to become involved in another phase of your life experience.

Here is an account of how one telephone call in advocacy for someone powerless helped to change her situation and to ease her pain:

I had interviewed Dodie in 1990. She was then 68, arthritic, recently widowed and recovering through AA for some 20 years. We had had no contact for nearly two years when one Sunday evening several months ago I received a telephone call from her. Since our interview, she told me, her arthritis had worsened, necessitating her move to sheltered care. She entered a nursing home selected by a stepson who lived in another state. The home was chosen, she believed, on the basis of what her Social Security benefits would allow and its geographical proximity to her former residence.

It happened, Dodie told me, that the nursing home was overcrowded and understaffed. Another factor in this crisis was Dodie's lack of advocacy. Several weeks prior to her telephone call to me, Dodie had been informed that she would have to move temporarily to a smaller space because her room was being converted to accommodate two people, sisters who wished to live together and who were coming to the home that very afternoon. Dodie, wishing to be cooperative, complied immediately, willing to undergo some inconvenience for the sake of the two sisters, who needed to be together. "I knew if I had a sister," she explained, "I sure would have wanted to be with her in this place."

What Dodie did not know, however, was that she would be placed "overnight" in a room without a window, a room that had formerly served as a broom closet. "Well, it really is a little bigger than my broom closet at home," conceded Dodie, not wishing to be unfair, "but it has been three weeks, and I still do not have a room with a window. I can get along without much space, but I do need light, don't you think?" she asked timidly.

She told me a bare light bulb hung suspended from the ceiling, in the middle of this tiny room that was barely large enough for a narrow cot. As Dodie described her situation to me, I was remembering a nursing home I had visited just a fortnight previously in the same state, Ohio. The rooms were spacious with modern shining oak furniture, and great windows overlooked picturesque, pastoral landscapes. Every resident slept on a three-quarter bed. Residents planned their own meals, and intergenerational living was the administrators' plan of the future.

On Monday morning I telephoned the administrator of the nursing home where Dodie was being held in her close, dark prison. He sounded both cordial and concerned, as he heard my complaint regarding Dodie's perplexing predicament. "Now, that's on the second floor," he began. "I'm not sure who's in charge of that wing." But before he could demur or dawdle further, I interrupted, "Oh, yes. I'm sure you know." And then all my years of assertiveness training and strengths as an advocate were, mercifully, with me. I heard myself uttering one simple sentence that included three magic words: "report . . . health authorities."

When I returned to my office on Tuesday morning, I heard Dodie's happy voice, lilting and chanting, on my answering machine. "I've got a room with a window . . . I've got a room with a window," she sang.

Every woman needs to prepare for those golden years. The older co-dependent woman who is not in recovery will have difficulty as characteristics of the disease tangle with a challenging reality. Already feeling abandoned, the unrecovering co-dependent woman will feel even more so as society increasingly turns its back on her, from her grown children who rarely come to visit to strangers who consider older women generally to be invisible nonentities. The unrecovering older woman, long leery of authority figures, will suddenly be surrounded by them in such forms as doctors, Social Security bureaucrats and nursing-home functionaries. Problems she experiences with self-esteem will lead her to believe that she deserves whatever kind of treatment she gets, good or bad, attentive or neglectful.

The attitudes and character traits of co-dependency make the unrecovering older woman a pushover in situations where others may not have her best interests at heart. It is vital that an older woman carry high self-esteem and possess a sense of who she is and what she wants. It is essential, then, that the older co-dependent woman be in recovery. She must be able to assert her needs. At the very least, she must make considered arrangements for someone to take care of things for her. And she must devise her plans and make her moves now and not procrastinate, that common trait of persons raised in dysfunctional households.

Facing Physical Realities

One of the issues of all co-dependent people is that of not being real. We deny our reality. We hear our friends complaining about their childish aging parents who refuse to accept their growing physical helplessness. This is difficult, but unless we take responsibility for our transitions, our decisions will have to be made for us. If a woman has fallen repeatedly, broken her bones, is unable to maintain her own body and still insists she is able to live alone, she is behaving irresponsibly and is likely to be excluded from making alternative choices for her future.

As aging women we need to be real about the many aspects of our mortality. To be perfectly blunt, what I'm talking about is dying.

Fear Of Dying

Everybody is going to die. This is a fact of life some of us don't want to face. I remember when I was about five years old, my mother told me that I was going to die someday. One of my older relatives had died, and I had gone with my family to the funeral. When we came back home, I was filled with questions.

I remember my mother saying that someday she would die and that I would die, too. Having no concept of what that meant in terms of growing up, aging and then dying, I went out crying. I went out to the chicken yard, where my friends were the chickens. I sat on the ground with my back up against the chicken fence in the dust and the dirt, crying about my own mortality, crying because I didn't want to die, and I certainly didn't want my mother to die. This was a very traumatic lesson for me.

Although my awful fear might have been eased had my mother shared with me her own feelings about death, I feel fortunate to have had so candid a mother. Frank discussion of death has become taboo in much of our culture. Through this shroud of secrecy, every aging woman's impending death translates into embarrassment and shame, for she is prohibited from talking about it. No one else talks about her aging either — at least not with her. Relatives usually do their talking about her through cupped hands at one another's ears. With death viewed as frightening and macabre, she is more likely to participate in the denial that she is aging, misstating her age and rejecting her maturity and mortality.

But we *are* going to die, not of old age per se, but probably of illness. It is a myth that people die of old age. Contrary to the attitude of the medical system in our country, aging itself is not a disease. We may, however, die of age-related diseases that overwhelm our elderly immune system, such as pneumonia, or from the debilitating consequences of smoking cigarettes or a lifetime spent reclining on a couch watching television and eating chocolate-covered cherries.

Fears Of The Age-Phobic

Just as old age is not a disease, neither are the physical changes that occur naturally during our aging process. Some exercise gurus and other age-phobic folks would have us believe that we can stay forever young but this is an impossible dream. For the recovering older woman, being realistic and practical about our aging bodies is as vital to our mental and physical health as regular exercise and good eating habits. In the dangerous denial of aging many submit themselves to further losses — denying, for instance, that they are having hearing difficulties and so not buying the hearing aid that could easily remedy the problem. Many older women, unwilling to admit that they are aging, do not seek to find out why they have specific aches or sudden shocks of pain and ultimately sink into a serious condition that may have been avoided.

We must admit that we are aging. From wrinkling skin to bones growing more brittle, every one of us undergoes physical changes as we age, changes that may at first alarm us. They are, however, an irrevocable fact of life. Only through accepting this process and the limitations it imposes upon us can we, paradoxically, better nurture ourselves through diet, vitamin and mineral supplements and exercise, to find our peace of mind.

The aging process differs from person to person, as do the ways we develop to cope with it. We need to stay in touch with our body's unique response to food and exercise. Some of us may find that we digest our food with a bit of difficulty, requiring that we eat smaller meals more frequently or stay away from certain foods that do not agree with us. Some of us, feeling halting and inflexible, will need to do a few minutes of daily stretches or yoga upon rising in the morning. On a mental level some of us may need to accept that our attention span is growing shorter. This process I call self-discernment, to accept these changes, rather than to complain about them. They are simply a part of who we are as precious beings growing older.

Some of our physical losses are, I believe, part of a natural order that transcends earthly concerns and takes us to higher realms. There may be, for instance, good reason for the gradual loss of our eyesight: perhaps we are not intended to focus on the minutiae of the physical plane as we age, but rather to enhance our spiritual development. In the dimming of our vision we are able to perceive the larger picture better, the psychosocial mural rather than the miniscule details of a single portrait.

Fear Of Senility

Many women during the interviewing described their terror of senility. I believe that senescence has a bad rap, that some lessening of our memory does occur — but we don't have to be over 55 for this to happen. In my own experience sometimes my memory goes, and sometimes it comes back. These variations may be something that we need to adjust to rather than hide from. For my part I'm not going to worry about it. Overall, it is a myth that cognitive impairment accompanies aging. When so many women say that they very much fear getting Alzheimer's, I tell them that as long as we can keep our minds active in positive ways and keep ourselves functioning and growing, as long as we demonstrate control over our lives, feeling engaged and free, expressing both our negative and positive emotions as they are with us in the moment, we are going to have less chance of developing Alzheimer's disease and other similar impairments.

Senescence as pathology may, in fact, be a metaphysical rather than strictly a physical phenomenon, the nerve cells of our brains short-circuiting with unresolved conflict. It could be that Alzheimer's has as its metaphysical connection the recollection in the older person of childhood abuse. Returning to thoughts of an abusive childhood, an older woman may find herself uncontrollably angry yet unable to express it. In some cases the feelings may be there even without the memory.

One of my interview subjects, the daughter of a physically abusive father, said that her mother, whose father had died of alcoholism, died of Alzheimer's disease. Was she, I inquired, a controlling person? No, her daughter replied, it was all wonderful. They had the most marvelous family. Except when her father was drunk, and these were rare occasions, never could she remember anything unpleasant in their household. There was never any problem, never any fighting. She never saw anything. Except when he was drunk. Hers was, I recognized, a family living in "white violence" during her father's periods of abstinence, where the undercurrent of conflict was ignored, where nothing was said because it was deemed unspeakable.

People from such families tend to live their adult lives in equally strict silence, avoiding conflict of any kind, firmly suppressing their feelings. It may very well be that in this rigid control, unexpressed resentment or rage becomes manifest as Alzheimer's disease. Like a dammed river that uncontrollably floods its riverbank elsewhere along its route, blocked feelings from blocked memories may wreak havoc on unsuspecting portions of our brains and, through our aging, at last find an outlet.

It is not a new thought that unexpressed emotion will display itself in physical illness. A great many older people have never been able to feel their feelings, let alone express them. Instead, they constantly exhibit their surgical scars, boils, sores, openings, fistulas, skin eruptions, falling-out hair or broken limbs. Such expressions of physical distress are considered socially acceptable, apparently, while emotional hurts are not. It is important to acknowledge this in recovery. No matter how old we are, it is never too late to become aware of blocked feelings, to identify them, to express them and hence to prevent disease.

Need For Nurture

It is also important that we lovingly nurture our bodies as we age. One aspect of this is touching and being touched. Every living cell has a memory that, in aging people, becomes lonely when left untouched. It is essential, then, that we touch ourselves, rub our hands across our bodies. One massage therapist told me that her clientele consists largely of older women. "For many of them, this is the only time all week that they are touched," she said. We need to have our hair brushed, our necks massaged, our hands and feet rubbed. These nonsexual gestures are essential in prolonging life and satisfy our hungry skin. Women can do this for each other.

Another significant note on nurturing: The older woman needs to designate trustworthy persons as advocates for her physical health, ranging from friends and relatives to nurses and doctors. One needs to keep in mind, too, that doctors are widely varied in their qualifications. As in any profession there are good ones and bad ones, careful ones and irresponsible ones. We must be conscientious in the selection of our healers. Getting second and third opinions on everything from periodontal work to hip replacement surgery needs to be a standard procedure.

Ultimately each of us must find our own way to care for our aging bodies. I know that I need to take special care of the right side of my body, the side that has a bad ankle, that lost a breast and that has a knee problem. I take care of myself in a tub of hot water, taking a kind of guided tour from my left side to my right, doing an exericise ritual that brings both sides of my body together. I do this through visualization, guided imagery, traveling to all parts of my body, emptying out any toxicity I find along the way.

Through the crown chakra at the top of my head, I take in gold-white light, circulating it in a clockwise motion all through my body. Every corner, every crevice, every muscle, every cell, every capillary is immersed and bathed in this healing universal connection of energy that is gold-white light. Gently it urges out any toxicity that it comes upon, moving down into my extremities in a circular motion, down into my ankles and feet, draining out through imagined spigots in the tips of my toes. Finally, after closing the spigots and making sure my body is filled with the cleansing healing light, I am on my way again.

Nursing Homes

> It's so crowded in my room at the nursing home, I don't even have room to change my mind! — Carrie, 84

Sooner or later, as we grow increasingly older and less able to take complete care of ourselves, many of us will need serious help from others. Interestingly, aging men generally receive care from women, either their daughters or their spouses. A great many women over the age of 65 provide round-the-clock care for ill husbands at home. Women in need of such care themselves, however, more frequently than men, enter nursing homes.

It is not too early to do our planning. There are choices to be made, needs to be asserted, caution to be taken, in making sure we live always in a healthy, nonabusive situation.

Unfortunately many an unrecovering woman, submissive by nature of her role in society and accustomed to abuse, finds herself in a nursing home where emotional or physical abuse is common. Part of every older woman's recovery is demanding good treatment while she is still mobile and alert and able to take care of herself. Many of the women I interviewed talked adamantly about how they don't want to be like their mother or father, dumped in a nursing home where nobody even visited them. We don't need to be.

This is certainly not to say that all nursing homes are "death houses," as generations gone by have named them. I have visited 16 nursing homes over the past two years and have observed many disparities among them. They run full scale, from dirty and dangerous warehouses for the elderly, to excellent, clean, professional, wonderfully warm and happy homes. A woman needs to be investigative in choosing an appropriate home. Perhaps she can enlist the help of an advocate to find a suitable place to live. Better yet, she may decide to remain in her own home, if that is possible, for as long as she can.

An important aside here: Some aging women who are recovering from perpetrating abuse on their own children must now be cautious to avoid abuse from those children. Remember, what we learn, we do and we teach. Statistics reveal to us that parents who were verbally, sexually or physically abusive to their family members are more likely to be abused by their former victims as they advance in age. Abusers must take responsibility for their behavior. As they recover they need to make amends, but they must also make it clear to their families that the abuse occurred in the presence of the disease of chemical dependence or co-dependence, and that they will not perpetrate abuse or tolerate abuse by others.

As we plan how and where we will live in our old age, we consider also the kinds of services we need, from Meals on Wheels to visiting nurses to shopping services. We need to explore to what extent we may expect families, friends and even neighbors to help us. We need to consider what we can afford and what kinds of financial assistance will realistically be provided us. We need to think about the neighborhood we live in, if we are in a safe or high-crime area or if we are physically isolated from or close to friends or family and recovery support.

Precious moments of a woman's life are going to be spent in the environment that she chooses for her golden years. She needs to be able to say things like, "I want a place where I can continue to play bridge, where I can cook my own meals. I want a place where I can have men around me, I don't want an all-women residence. I like the company of the opposite sex. I want a place where I can continue my dancing, where I can swim, where I can quilt and so on. I want a place where I can tour the countryside on buses. I want a place where I can get vegetarian meals." Whatever she dreams of, she needs to say she wants to have.

Central to all considerations is that she find a place that supports her continued recovery. During the course of interviewing I met several women who at one time in their lives had been able to reach out to people but who now find themselves isolated, confined to wheelchairs or otherwise immobile in nursing homes, thereby having lost the support of such groups as Al-Anon and AA. Theirs is a perilous place to be.

The Recovering Alcoholic In A Nursing Home

A recovering alcoholic in a nursing home needs ongoing support in order to stay sober. She must never forget that she has a chronic illness that keeps her just one drink away from getting drunk. We must inform our caregivers and medical attendants that we are alcoholic — or at least tell them that we are allergic to alcohol, the word that the general public understands. They must know that we cannot drink alcohol or anything with alcohol in it. Furthermore, we cannot take Valium or such mood-altering medications as antidepressants unless they are something we are familiar with and know exactly how to monitor.

Ironically, in asserting our needs, we may find ourselves at odds with doctors and other health-care professionals. But once again, we must not imperil ourselves and our recovery by placing ourselves in the hands of a medical person, simply because the letters M.D. or Ph.D. follow his or her name. We must take a careful look at the overall care a nursing home offers. Some are greatly lacking in the resources required to offer quality care to their residents. The cost of a nursing home, incidentally, does not necessarily correlate with the quality of its care. For an excellent consumer's perspective on nursing homes, refer to the Addendum, which includes descriptions of quality care by nursing-home residents themselves

and is published by the National Citizens Coalition for
Nursing Home Reform.

Moving Into A Nursing Home

With foresight and careful planning, moving into a nursing home or other sheltered care can be the beginning of
a satisfying new stage of life. This transition may be an
emotionally trying one, however. Selling one's home and
moving can be for some tantamount to relinquishing all of
life's memories. To ease the burden of transition I suggest
the following: write your life's story by the decades, ages 1
to 10, 10 to 20 and so on. Then, from each era choose one
object that holds special meaning for you — a piece of
clothing, perhaps, or a doll or a trinket. Gather these seven
or eight items together, these precious mementos, each a
symbol of an important decade of your life, and carry them
with you, knowing that wherever you go, your history will
live with you.

Money

A brief but important note about money: No matter
how much or how little money she has, the aging woman
needs to keep an eye on it. Learning how to manage her
own money, if she does not already do so, can be one of
the most self-empowering acts an older woman will ever
perform. Many women are thrilled in their retirement or
widowhood to be managing their own finances. One of
my older friends even went so far as to enroll in an evening course in finance at a graduate school of business.

"I don't have very much money," she said, "but I'm
going to make sure that I know what's happening to
what I do have."

Unfortunately, most women have been taught that they
are incapable of understanding financial or business matters. What's more, these women believe that all they possess rightly belongs to their spouses, who are then obliged
to take care of them. The woman who has not addressed

this issue risks exploitation. Specifically widows and divorced women newly in recovery are fair game for fraudulent practices.

Few situations present a more heart-rending scene than the older woman who has been swindled by the man she loves. This is not as uncommon as one may think. Women who are bilked of their savings by con men who court and rob them are finally breaking through their embarrassment and coming forward to tell their stories of misadventure and emotional susceptibility.

In one affluent community in Vermont, for example, a woman reported having found two other women over the age of 60 who had wed the same man with whom she also had exchanged marriage vows. She had lived with him for a year, then divorced him after she discovered that he had bilked her of $45,000 and a Lincoln Town Car. These were, by the way, recovering women. All three met this man at AA meetings and related social functions. It appears that he had ascertained that those older women, newly in recovery from alcoholism, were easy targets. In total, the three women he married concluded that he had made off with a quarter of a million dollars.

A few warning signs offered by these older women may help others to avoid involving themselves in relationships with such men. Among them: He initiates courtship flamboyantly, lavishing attention and gifts upon you, yet quickly tapering off to wanting "just to be home alone with you." He speaks of living well but presents no evidence of it. He does not allow you out of his sight, and he knows where you are and with whom you are at all times. He wants to marry you as soon as possible. He has been looking for you for a lifetime and does not want to waste another minute.

Romantic this person may be, but a woman's selection of a potential intimate partner requires building trust through patience and time. Being cautious is both prudent and judicious, not paranoid.

Remaining Useful

Irrefutable is that the recovering woman must continue to feel valuable as she grows older. Throughout the interviews the women who were the most enthusiastic about their longevity were those who felt themselves to be useful. Being useful here does not mean merely being constantly occupied but contributing to the world. Again and again the women talked of the value of being valuable.

We find our bliss in contributing to the world rather than being passive participants. Sometimes I think, well, I really want to go to my farm and just stay there forever. But I also know that what keeps me alive, challenged and enthusiastic is my work. So I continue to spend weekends on my farm and weekdays back in the city, working with my clients.

Others have made similar decisions to keep going. "If I cannot make a contribution, then why am I here? If I can't keep being useful, I might as well fold up and say 'good afternoon,'" said Sadie, 84, bending over the duffle bag she was packing for her travels to the Southwest to participate in another Elder Hostel archaeological dig.

And then there's Peg, who stood in the sunlight among the forsythia beside her home and art studio as she spoke with me, her wispy white hair pulled back from her high forehead, bright yellow splotches of paint dotting her denim pants:

> I'm 72 and I have never been happier. I am useful. I certainly don't feel old, at least not as I was taught what "old" means. I am free of alcohol, at least for today, and I am free of my husband's Alzheimer's. I miss Roy, but I feel great relief in not having to take care of him. I have all the parts I was born with, including my teeth. Three weeks ago I had a cataract removed, and I was astonished to learn I had been looking through something similar to a glass of iced tea. And my art is at last gaining national recognition! [Her fans know her for the multicolored squares she paints on furniture and doors, a technique that has become her trademark.] When I was a child in an alcoholic home, when

the chaos got to be unbearable, I would walk up and down the front hall and count the black and white blocks of marble in the floor. Then I was able to shut out the screaming and the violence. Now, today, that block image has become a vital part of my art. I feel sorry for some of the other older widows in recovery who have no interests other than AA. I am so grateful for my art. It keeps me growing and productive.

As our supply of days and years diminishes, our lives become more priceless. Our years, our days, our moments become more valuable. For me, going into my 64th year, I look at the countryside every weekend as I drive to my home, savoring the springtime flowing softly into summer, the shades of vibrant green changing into autumn's yellow and rust, the death of fall and then the deep grey that blends softly into winter with its cloak of reassuring snow. And then back again into spring, with green life teeming everywhere. Each time I experience this cycle, seeing the comings and the goings of the seasons, I know that I am aging, that these rare and rich moments of joy are becoming fewer and fewer.

We all need to acknowledge this special time, going gently into death, giving love and respect to the people around us and to the Earth, which is Mother of us all.

Diana

Diana has been recovering from breast cancer for seven years. She is 57 years old. Diana is also in recovery from co-dependence. After her double mastectomy, she began to see a therapist. With that therapist Diana began to believe that breast cancer has to do with not having been nurtured as a child. She believes, too, that her cancer was related to having had her own nurturing instincts blocked. We began working together to remove the blocks of mal-energy that had caused her cancer, caused the tumors.

Diana continues to visualize the healing flow of energy throughout her body. She understands and believes that, through her changing how she relates to other people, friends and family members, not needing any longer to harbor resentment, having expressed her anger and rage appropriately to some of her long-dead ancestors, she is healing; she's getting well. By recovering from co-dependent belief systems she believes that she is preventing the cancer process. One day at a time. The cancer has not returned over this period. And as she said, "I don't feel like anything's eating at me anymore."

CHAPTER NINE

Spirituality, Good Spirits And Affirmations

In recovery we feel tremendously fortunate to be able to co-create and develop many loving and trustworthy friendships. We feel blessed to choose to generate a wonderful family over isolation or remaining limited by the painful roots of our families of origin. Over the years many friends and acquaintances, even people younger than I, have died. Still others come. In making my choices I am grateful to have had the guidance of a Higher Power. This Power has been manifest in the helping hands of many people, most of them women, who have been my mentors and my supporters, gently prodding and pulling me along my path.

This Power is also within me, the spirit that is myself. Looking back on my childhood I see the value of the role that I played in my family, painful though it was. Lost and lonely, even as a child I needed to reach out to others, but untrusting, I could rarely do that. Instead I discovered within myself creative abilities and a perseverance that bolstered and sustained me through many trying times. I became a child who was willing to take risks, who moved beyond the confines of the refrains, "No, you can't" and "You are bad," from those various relatives who felt burdened by my presence in the world after I was orphaned. The splendid spirit of my surviving child within is with me still.

My spirituality is my energy, my thought processes, my values. It is ever-changing, ever-evolving. My spirituality is my connection with the world and the way I am in the world. Since the birth of my recovery I no longer have the sense of living lonely in a fishbowl, algae growing all around me while I peek out at a bewildering world through a tiny opening, isolated and barely able to see. In my growing spirituality I experience myself as an integral and valuable part of my world, of my universe. I feel full of wonder . . . wonderful.

A Sacred Place

One practical aspect of my spirituality has been establishing a sacred place. To that end came the natural and slow creation of an altar in a corner of my house, which has been growing and changing wherever I have lived since the beginning of my sobriety, 22 years ago. Without a named purpose, my altar simply began as a small covered table and a chair where I sat to burn candles to send healing energy to an ill friend. I began to read there, to pray there, to meditate there. I brought my most meaningful keepsakes there. It became the matrix for symbols of my universe: a feather representing the air we breathe; crystals and little stones from the earth; candles, like the sun, carrying light and fire; and always the little vessel of water. These are the four basic elements of which we are made.

It is my holy place, where I store my most meaningful souvenirs. Many women have created such altars, and I highly recommend it. Please know that constructing an altar is a reverent gesture. It is not apostasy. Some women adorn their altars with pictures of their families, of their Higher Power. I have seen altars with mezuzahs, crucifixes, prayer rugs, crystals, stones, pyramids, wild turkey feathers, headbands, yarn sculptures, lavender lace, wildflowers, books of affirmations, mandalas, tintypes of grandmothers' grandmothers. Some women adorn their altars with hanging plants, murals and mirrors. These are the keepsakes of our lives. Our altars change as we change. They become reminders of who we are in all our beloved aspects.

The Wise Woman Within

Central to my spirituality is what I call my Wise Woman Within. She provides the answers to the very mysteries of life and death and regeneration.

In the 1960s a woman street singer in Washington, D.C. used to sing a song called "Good Old Dora," a song about the Wise Woman Within. She sang about how this woman watched over her, how she was her best counsel and support.

The Wise Woman of this song was, in essence, self-love. She resides within each of us, women and men alike. She represents what some consider common sense, a combination of intuition and choice-making in action. The Wise Woman Within symbolizes for each of us the loving mother-child bond, that primordial model for all human relationships. In its ideal form it is the perfect paradigm of giving and receiving, the foundation of growth toward the very peak of human consciousness.

My Wise Woman Within is my spiritual creativity at work. She is noble and strong, operating by a code of honor that our culture has largely reserved for men: she is a hero, my heroine. Formidable but nonviolent, she is always ready with her spiritual magic to protect the vulnerable child. Every one of us possesses her, this loving advocate who knows that every injustice against a child, every cruel word and gesture, is undeserved.

My Wise Woman Within was the one who spoke to me long ago: "You will survive," she said. "At some point you will make choices." She is the one who told me that some day I would love myself and that others would love me. She was the one who led me down a gravel road to a neighbor's house a mile away from home one hot summer morning when I was four years old, to knock timidly on Mrs. Althoff's back screen door, to ask her if she would have a little time that morning to hold me on her lap.

My Wise Woman Within kept me out of harm's way, even as I fled more deeply into my alcoholism. And when the time came to take the big risk of sobriety, she was with me still. She was the one who spoke to me after I drunkenly smashed my car into 10 cars on February 18, 1970, and I woke up bruised and with stitches in my mouth and tongue, my body swollen from the battering I had given myself in that last binge. She was the one whose quiet voice I heard say, "It's over, that part is over. You're okay now." It was the Wise Woman Within who watched over me as I inflicted that last deep pain in my brain before I could at last cast off the addiction. Like a guardian angel she came knocking with her wake-up call.

My Wise Woman Within gives me the courage to stand up confidently before doubting questioning peers, clients, family, even community. She is the one who tells me, "Helen, you know what's good for you."

It was she who unerringly directed me to my little pocket of paradise in Wisconsin. She directs me every day of my working life, is with me and my clients as we join in our struggle together. She is the one who helps me to reach out to others and allows me to be touched by them.

The visionary Earth Mother, the Wise Woman Within, unseen has graced the world since the dawn of time. She possesses great powers to transcend traditional, unworkable concepts within the individual and society, to overcome hindrances in understanding and communication among all people. The extraordinary transformations inherent in our recovery become more possible through her power. With her help we can move mountains. She heals our sorrows, challenges us to move beyond fear, offers us renewal and regeneration and promises us serenity, contentment and peace.

I make contact with my Wise Woman Within through creative visualization. A brief meditative type of exercise that I do may put you in touch with your own Wise Woman Within:

Sitting in a quiet private place, eyes closed, begin to focus on your breathing. Inhale deeply and exhale slowly. Know that with each inhalation you are taking into your body pure oxygen that cleanses and heals. With every exhalation know you are ridding your body of all the toxins that have gathered within on this day. With each breath inhale more deeply, until you inhale nearly to your genitals, and exhale slowly. As you grow increasingly calm you notice a sense of relaxation, a warm, gentle, flowing current, beginning to circulate throughout your body, starting at the base of your skull and floating downward in a circular, caressing motion. You begin to feel warm and relaxed. This relaxation energy flows slowly down and across your body as warm liquid. Now you begin to feel perfectly safe and lovable. As your deep and regular breathing continues the relaxation now flows throughout your body, to all parts, inside and outside, down to the very tips of your toes. Take as long as you need.

Totally relaxed and safe now, and feeling very lovable and loving, go inside your body and wait for your Wise Woman Within. She will come. Watch for her. Her form will begin to take shape. My own Wise Woman Within has long flowing grey hair and deep blue eyes. She is ancient, and she is dressed in a soft velvet robe lined with feathers. She wears precious stones around her neck. Her face is brown and beautiful, with deep lines. She is smiling.

If you feel like crying, it may be your hurting Child Within who is still in pain from years gone by. Find that child now, within you, and place her tenderly in the loving arms of your Wise Woman Within. Know that all of you is perfectly safe at this moment, and know that you are very lovable. Now allow your tears to come. These are healing tears. Try holding yourself with your arms around yourself, and perhaps rock yourself a little. There is comfort in this.

If you are jubilant, allow yourself to feel and express this joy with your Wise Woman Within. You may wish to do a little dance. Or give yourself a hug of joy! She is benevolent, your Wise Woman Within, and always ready with gentle counsel and comfort. Know that she is always available to you. If you lose contact, it is because you have forgotten her. She never forgets you. She is with you always.

Now come out of your meditation with a smile of gratitude. Today will be a good day.

My Wise Woman Within has grown older and more dear to me as I age. I urge you to get in touch with your own Wise Woman Within. Ask your questions and wait for her answers. They will come. And when they do, say thank you and tell her you love and appreciate her.

Remaining In Good Spirits

We hear a great deal these days about stress. No matter how far we are in our recovery, stress is something most of us need to work with. Fortunately there are steps one can take to reduce stress and increase one's sense of well-being and even happiness. A few of them:

- *Meditate.* Practice the kind of exercise described above. Perhaps you are convinced that you will not enjoy or benefit from meditation. I urge you to try it anyway. Or if you would prefer, consider enrolling in a class to learn how to meditate. You may be pleasantly surprised at the gift of calm and composure it offers.
- *Get a massage.* Basic Swedish massage with its long, flowing strokes is a perfect tension-reliever. But many other kinds of bodywork are effective, too, from deep tissue manipulation to gentle acupressure. Read about them, talk to people who have tried

them and treat yourself to the experience. You may even want to learn how to *give* massage; then barter that skill.

- *Exercise.* Some older women who have led sedentary lives have been astounded to discover after the age of 55 that exercise is transforming to body, mind and spirit. A number of women I interviewed told me that they took up swimming after they retired, sometimes after they had moved into a residential setting equipped with a swimming pool. I love to take long, invigorating walks daily in the hills around my farm and to the lake when I am in the city. *Daily* is the operative term here.

- *Spend time with nature.* I climbed trees when I was a girl, and today I climb the burr oaks on my farm. Nestled in the branches, I write poetry or have imaginary conversations with people or chipmunks or deer or sometimes even with the leaves.

- *Learn something new.* We need never stop learning, especially in recovery when each day challenges us to change and grow. Sign up for a class in a subject you've always been interested in. Or try your hand at an artistic venture, from designing your own greeting cards to making candles from scratch (this is one of my favorite avocations). One woman I interviewed told me that she had always wanted to learn to ride a motorcycle but had been forbidden to do so by her husband. She finally learned at the age of 56 after her husband died.

- *Keep setting goals.* When you reach one goal, celebrate and then set another. Traditionally people have been expected to limit themselves as they age. Quite contrarily many of us have learned to spread out, amplify our capabilities and expand our horizons.

- *Save your positive strokes.* Over the last ten years I have saved three baskets of loving and supportive letters, notes and greeting cards from friends and clients. If I feel dejected, if a client is angry because of the confrontational nature of my work or if I find myself questioning my values or otherwise doubting myself, I go to these baskets and at random pick one of these cards, all of which tell me that I am wonderful. Try it yourself: keep a little store of cards and letters that are well-meaning and express positive regard for you, messages that are complimentary, supportive, warm and comforting. They can serve at times as a support group when one is not immediately available.

Affirmations

I have been recommending for years that my clients use affirmations. Some do so with skepticism, doubtful that the recital of a few positive words can make any difference in the way they feel about themselves and their world. But they do. Affirmations, as I describe them to my clients, are lies that we tell ourselves until they become our truths. They are not actually lies, but we often start out feeling that they are. Are we really beautiful, smart, capable, deserving people? Of course we are, but many of us have never heard this message from anyone and so we don't believe it in the beginning.

Affirmations are personal. They are also common and collective. They are important for the individual, our society, our planet. People making affirmations are putting into the world energy that can transform themselves and others in positive and powerful ways.

We need to do affirmations every day, sometimes aloud, sometimes silently, always vividly visualizing the state of being that we are describing. We draw energy to ourselves and send out energy for those who have been rendered disadvantaged and disenfranchised. In this way all of us older recovering women can help our sisters.

I have literally hundreds of affirmations, some gleaned from readings, some heard from other people, many of my own invention. The point is to be creative in formulating them. Please, tailor your own affirmations to your unique needs. Some of my favorites are:

I live in the now. Every moment is a new moment.

I release all resentments that I have of the past. I move forward with love in my heart.

I am safe and free within my boundaries.

I am a wise woman filled with light and love.

I love all the parts of my body.

I love my aging body.

I love my mind and the lovely memories it chooses to keep.

I have the right to ask for what I want.

I choose to love and to enjoy myself.

Today I am my own authority, for I am the only one who is inside of my mind.

I rejoice in the uniqueness of others.

I am growing with each passing day.

I transform all my experiences into insurance that I am safe.

I impact my life force on the world through my aging process.

I am willing to share all my secrets.

I have a long list to unlearn.

The best facelift is my smile.

I relieve my body of all tension and stress from worry about others. I send them loving, healing energy.

I work my life. I work my process as I work my daily tasks.

As I make financial and emotional amends through the resolution of my conflicts, I feel my worth as a woman.

My Older is younger now than my Older used to be.

As an aging woman I have a great "earned surplus."

I am no longer a black-and-white person. I am grey!

With all that I have been and all that I am, I am becoming all that I can be.

I belong. And I shall always belong.

Today I give myself all the credit I need. I deserve much more, of course, but today I give myself all that I need.

My wants and needs are similar and are growing closer to being the same with every new day.

I am proud to be a woman, open and older.

I deserve all that I want and need.

I am a member of the human circle.

With each healing day the destructive patterns of my life slip away. I am getting clear.

Forgiveness for me is the icing on the cake; it is not the cake mix.

I accept all that has happened to me and through me, to help to build the "new" me.

I am so proud of my aging loveliness. I have earned every wrinkle, every grey hair.

At the top of the hill is where I sit as an older woman, courageously and proudly, atop it.

I am enough.

I am.

Fable

Once upon a time there was a cruel and powerful king who conquered many lands simply by cutting off his victims' food supply. One day he laid siege to a village. It was a peaceful and happy village that for centuries had had no cause to fear attack from any enemy and so was not prepared with weapons to fight back. When the king's army surrounded the town and allowed no one to leave, all the men of the town, having been forever free to come and go as they pleased, believed they were lost and doomed to die.

"We shall perish," they moaned, "for unless we are free to go outside the village for berries from the forest and fish from the river nearby, we shall all soon starve." And they prepared to surrender to the enemy.

Then the older women of the village, who knew a fair amount about dealing with constrictions and lack of freedom, began talking with each other. "If we can escape into the dense forest," they reasoned, "we shall be safe, for we know all the nooks and crannies to hide in. Then we can escape to another land and get on with our lives." And while the men sat crouched and motionless with their arms in the air, the women talked with each other in a great circle throughout the afternoon.

That evening the women all went together to speak to the king. "Oh, mighty Sire," they begged. "We are aware that you are proud to be a wise and fair king. Grant us, then, the one favor of allowing us, the women of this village, to leave with our children, carrying with us only those things that are the most fragile and precious."

Indeed, the king often boasted that he lived by his wits and had never broken an agreement. Now he became amused by these deranged and powerless women and even more amused at their naive proposition because he knew the town was poor and had no treasures. He granted the women permission, therefore, to leave the village with their children. "Women and children may leave as agreed," he decreed. "But if any man attempts to disguise himself as a woman and is found trying to walk out of this village, all of you will die!"

The next morning at dawn the gates of the village opened wide to let the women and children through. The older children scurried ahead, the women following with infants in their arms . . . each woman carrying one man on her back.

The End

Appendix 1

Power Of Attorney Over Health

The recovering woman has to consider long-term-care insurance, whether or not she would like a living will and upon whom she would like to bestow the power of attorney. Seminars on these subjects are offered in most nursing and residential homes. The public is also usually invited to attend, so watch for these.

It is important that the recovering older woman know her state's laws regarding her right to refuse medical care as a competent person and her right to leave a hospital if she is not satisfied with it. She has a right, for instance, to refuse to be examined by medical students, interns or residents in any hospital anywhere. Many people are not aware of this. The older woman needs to know her rights in the event that she has an accident, whether a hospital can turn her away (it can), and that once she is admitted, the hospital cannot send her away.

Following is a sample of an agreement for designating someone with the power of attorney. Please note that the legal details of the power of attorney over health may vary from state to state. Our example comes from the state of Wisconsin. Should you wish to put such a document into effect, please check with your state of residence for its official requirements.

Power Of Attorney For Health-Care Document

Notice To Person Making This Document

You have the right to make decisions about your health care. No health care may be given to you over your objection, and necessary health care may not be stopped or withheld if you object.

Because your health-care providers in some cases have not had the opportunity to establish a long-term relationship with you, they are often unfamiliar with your beliefs and values and the details of your family relationships. This poses a problem if you become physically or mentally unable to make decisions about your health care.

In order to avoid this problem you may sign this legal document to specify the person whom you want to make health-care decisions for you if you are unable to make those decisions personally. That person is known as your health-care agent. You should take some time to discuss your thoughts and beliefs about medical treatment with the person or persons whom you have specified. You may state in this document any types of health care that you do or do not desire, and you may limit the authority of your health-care agent as you wish. If your health-care agent is unaware of your desires with respect to a particular health-care decision, he or she is required to determine what would be in your best interests in making the decision.

This is an important legal document. It gives the person whom you specify broad powers to make health-care decisions for you. It revokes any prior power of attorney for health care that you may have made. If you change your mind about whether a person should make health-care decisions for you, or about which person that should be, you may revoke this document at any time by destroying the document or by directing another person to destroy it in your presence, revoking it in a written statement that you sign and date or stating that it is revoked in the presence of two witnesses. If you revoke, you should notify the person you had specified, your health-care providers and any other person to whom you have given a copy. If the person you have specified is your spouse and your marriage is annulled or you are divorced after signing this document, the document is invalid.

Do not sign this document unless you clearly understand what it means.

It is suggested that you keep the original of this document on file with your physician.

Power Of Attorney For Health Care

Instrument made this _____ day of _____ (month), _____ (year).

Creation Of Power Of Attorney For Health Care

I, _____

_____ (name and address), being of sound mind, intend by this document to create a power of attorney for health care. My executing this power of attorney for health care is voluntary. I expect, despite the creation of this power of attorney for health care, to be fully informed about and allowed to participate in any health-care decision for me, to the extent that I am able. For the purposes of this document, "health-care decision" means an informed decision in the exercise of my right to accept, maintain, discontinue or refuse any care, treatment, service or procedure to maintain, diagnose or treat my physical or mental condition.

Designation Of Health-Care Agent

If I am no longer able to make health-care decisions for myself, due to my incapacity, I hereby designate _____

_____

_____ (name, address and telephone number) to be my health-care agent for the purpose of making health-care decisions on my behalf. Neither the health-care agent nor the alternative health-care agent whom I have designated is my health-care provider, an employee of my health-care provider or an employee of a health-care facility in which I reside or am a patient or a spouse of any of these persons, or, if he or she is that health-care provider or employee or spouse of that health-care provider or employee, he or she is also my relative. For purposes of this document "incapacity" exists if two physicians or a physician and a psychologist who have personally examined me sign a statement that specifically expresses their opinion that I have a condition that means that I am unable to receive and evaluate information effectively or communicate decisions to such an extent that I lack the capacity to manage my health-care decisions. A copy of that statement, if made, must be attached to this document.

GENERAL STATEMENT OF AUTHORITY GRANTED

Unless I have specified otherwise in this document, if I ever have incapacity, I instruct my health-care provider to obtain the health-care decision of my health-care agent for all of my health care. I have discussed my desires thoroughly with my health-care agent and believe that he or she understands my philosophy regarding the health-care decisions I would make if I were so able. I desire that my wishes be carried out through the authority given to my health-care agent under this document.

My health-care agent is instructed that if I am unable, due to my incapacity, to make a health-care decision, he or she shall make a health-care decision for me, except that in exercising the authority given to him or her by this document my health-care agent should try to discuss with me any specific proposed health care if I am able to communicate in any manner, including by blinking my eyes. If this communication cannot be made, my health-care agent shall base his or her health-care decision on any health-care choices that I have expressed prior to the time of the decision. If I have not expressed a health-care choice about the health care in question and communication cannot be made, my health-care agent shall base his or her health-care decision on what he or she believes to be in my best interest.

LIMITATIONS ON MENTAL HEALTH TREATMENT

My health-care agent may not admit or commit me on an inpatient basis to an institution for mental diseases, an intermediate-care facility for the mentally retarded, a state treatment facility or a county treatment facility. My health-care agent may not consent to experimental mental health research or psychosurgery, electroconvulsive treatment or other drastic mental health treatment procedures for me.

ADMISSION TO NURSING HOMES OR COMMUNITY-BASED RESIDENTIAL FACILITIES

My health-care agent may admit me to a nursing home or community-based residential facility for short-term stays for recuperative care or respite care.

If I am diagnosed as mentally ill or developmentally disabled, my health-care agent may not admit me to a nursing home or community-based residential facility for a purpose other than recuperative care or respite care.

If I am not diagnosed as mentally ill or developmentally disabled, and if I have checked Yes to the following, however, my health-care agent may admit me for a purpose other than recuperative care or respite care to:

1. A nursing home: Yes _____ No _____
2. A community-based residential facility:
   Yes _____ No _____

If I have not checked either Yes or No to admission to a nursing home or community-based residential facility for a purpose other than recuperative care or respite care, my health-care agent may only admit me for short-term stays for recuperative care or respite care.

PROVISION OF NUTRITION AND HYDRATION

If I have checked Yes to the following, my health-care agent may have non-orally ingested nutrition and hydration withheld or withdrawn from me, unless my physician has advised that, in his or her professional judgment, this will cause me pain or will reduce my comfort. If I have checked No to the following, my health-care agent may not have non-orally ingested nutrition and hydration withheld or withdrawn from me.

My health-care agent may not have orally ingested nutrition or hydration withheld or withdrawn from me unless provision of the nutrition or hydration is medically contraindicated.

Withhold or withdraw non-orally ingested nutrition and hydration: Yes _____ No _____.

If I have not checked either Yes or No to withholding or withdrawing non-orally ingested nutrition and hydration, my health-care agent may not have non-orally ingested nutrition and hydration withdrawn from me.

Inspection And Disclosure Of Information Relating To My Physical Or Mental Health

Subject to any limitations in this document, my health-care agent has the authority to do all of the following:

a. Request, review and receive any information, verbal or written, regarding my physical or mental health, including medical and hospital records.
b. Execute on my behalf any documents that may be required in order to obtain this information.
c. Consent to the disclosure of this information.

Signing Documents, Waivers And Releases

Where necessary to implement the health-care decisions that my health-care agent is authorized by this document to make, my health-care agent has the authority to execute on my behalf any of the following:

a. Documents titled or purporting to be a "Consent to Permit Treatment," "Refusal to Permit Treatment" or "Leaving Hospital Against Medical Advice."
b. A waiver or release from liability required by a hospital or physician.

Signature Of Principal

(Person creating the power of attorney for health care)
Signature _____

Statement Of Witnesses

I know the principal personally and I believe him or her to be of sound mind and at least 18 years of age. I believe that his or her execution of this power of attorney for health care is voluntary. I am at least 18 years of age and am not related to the principal by blood, marriage or adoption. I am not a health-care provider who is serving the principal at this time. To the best of my knowledge, I am not entitled to and do not have a claim on the principal's estate.

Witness #1 Print Name _____

Address _____

Signature _____ Date _____

Witness #2 Print Name _____

Address _____

Signature _____ Date _____

STATEMENT OF HEALTH-CARE AGENT

I understand that _____ (name of principal) has designated me to be his or her health-care agent if he or she is ever found to have incapacity and is unable to make health-care decisions himself or herself. _____ (name of principal) has discussed his or her desires regarding health-care decisions with me.

Signature _____

Address _____

STATEMENT OF ALTERNATE HEALTH-CARE AGENT

I understand that _____ (name of principal) has designated me to be his or her health-care agent if he or she is ever found to have incapacity and is unable to make health-care decisions himself or herself and if the person designated as health-care agent is unable or unwilling to make those decisions. _____ (name of principal) has discussed his or her desires regarding health-care decisions with me.

Signature _____

Address _____

Appendix 2

Last Will And Testament

Last Will and Testament of

_____

I, _____, of the city of _____,
_____ county, of the state of _____,
being now of sound and disposing mind and memory, do
hereby make, publish and declare this to be my last WILL,
revoking any and all former WILLS, CODICILS or other
TESTAMENTARY DISPOSITIONS made by me.

ONE. I authorize and direct my personal representative
to pay the expenses of my last illness and funeral and all
of my just debts as soon as practicable.

TWO. I give all of my property, of whatever kind and
wherever situated, to _____.

THREE. If any beneficiary dies before the entry of judgment distributing my property, or less than sixty (60)

days after my death, whichever is earlier, any interest that beneficiary would have had under the terms of this WILL is to be distributed in accordance with the provisions of this WILL as though that beneficiary had predeceased me.

FOUR. I appoint _____ as personal representative of my estate to serve without bond. If for any reason she or he does not so serve, I appoint _____, also to serve without bond.

FIVE. I give to my personal representative the full power and authority to sell and dispose of any and all of the property of which I die seized, at public or private sale, at such times and in such manner as he or she shall deem best, and to make all needful conveyances, deeds and transfers necessary to pass full, perfect and complete title to any part and the whole thereof; to collect and compromise all debts, demands and claims that may be due or owing, as well as any liabilities to which I or my estate may be subject. All decisions that he or she shall in good faith make concerning the inclusion or exclusion of particular property in my estate for federal estate tax purposes, the date for valuation of property for estate tax purposes, whether certain deductions shall be taken as income tax deductions or estate tax deductions, or any other questions related to the tax matters, shall be conclusive on all concerned and he or she shall not be liable to my estate or any of the beneficiaries hereunder for any losses occasioned by such decisions.

IN WITNESS WHEREOF, I have hereunto subscribed by hand to this, my LAST WILL AND TESTAMENT, this _____ day of _____, 19____.

_____ signature

The foregoing instrument, consisting of two and one-half (2½) typewritten pages, including this attestation page, was on the day of its executive, to wit: the _____ day of _____, 19____, duly signed and declared by _____, in our presence, and for her LAST WILL AND TESTAMENT, and we, at her request and in her presence and in the presence of each other, have hereunto subscribed our names and post office addresses as attesting witnesses; and we do further state that at the time of execution of this WILL, said testatrix was of sound and disposing mind and memory and laboring under no undue influence of any kind.

_____ signature of _____ city,
STATE

_____ signature of _____ city,
STATE

_____ signature of _____ city,
STATE

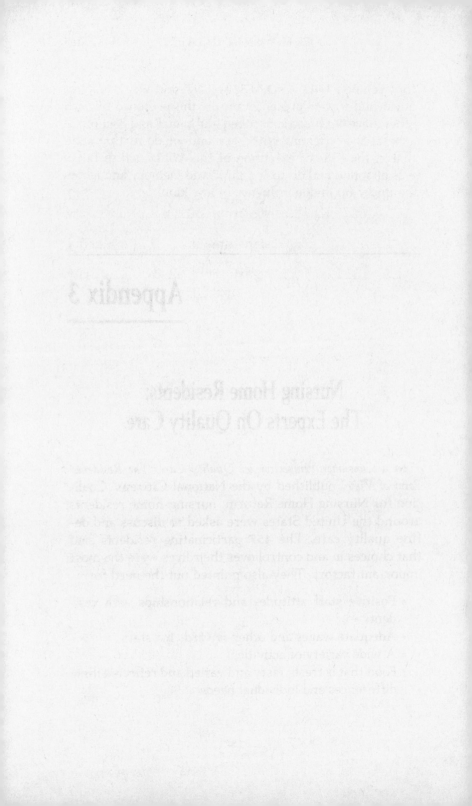

Appendix 3

Nursing Home Residents: The Experts On Quality Care

In a *Consumer Perspective on Quality Care: The Residents' Point of View*, published by the National Citizens' Coalition for Nursing Home Reform, nursing-home residents around the United States were asked to discuss and define quality care. The 457 participating residents said that choices in and control over their lives were the most important factors. They also pointed out the need for:

- Positive staff attitudes and relationships with residents
- Adequate wages and other rewards for staff
- A wide variety of activities
- Food that is fresh, tasty and varied and reflects ethnic differences and individual needs

- Explicit, workable channels for problem resolution (accompanied by love and understanding)
- Safety of the environment
- Maximum possible independence for residents
- Strong, enforced regulations
- Resident participation in policymaking and quality control, both in their own facility and at state and federal levels
- An active, concerned, informed administrator
- Community involvement.

Appendix 4

Nutrition And The Older Recovering Woman

Contributed by Dr. Nancy Katz

Very few medical clinicians are trained in the nutritional needs of the elderly and/or persons in recovery, and even fewer are trained in the needs of the elderly in recovery, so the weight of health rests on you as one of these individuals. Out of necessity it is your responsibility to pick the brain, if you will, of your health-care providers and to read and learn as much as you can about your own nutritional needs and how best to meet them. In making this effort, not only will you be improving your health, but you will also be influencing the health-care system to acknowledge the very real need for education in the field of nutrition, the elderly and recovery.

Carbohydrates

The majority of calories in the American diet come from carbohydrates. Unfortunately, as has been known for years, as we age our ability to metabolize carbohydrates decreases. So to maintain a good level of health as we age, we should reduce the amount of simple carbohydrates (sugar, candy, cakes, cookies, etc.) and increase the amount of complex carbohydrates (whole grains, oats, wheat, barley, etc.). This will help to reduce the symptoms of hyperglycemia or hypoglycemia — high or low blood sugar levels — that many elderly people experience, such as sweating, progressive confusion and irritation. Such a change in diet will also aid in bowel motility and resolve constipation.

Protein

While generally we think that the elderly need less protein than younger people, in truth they may require more protein due to the fact that their metabolism is not so efficient as it once was. Another issue regarding dietary protein is renal kidney disease. Renal function progressively declines after the age of 30. By the time a person is in their 80s, the filtration rate is one-half to one-third what it previously was. It has also been shown that dietary restriction of protein early in the course of renal disease will slow the progress of the disease. Since alcohol consumption causes damage to the kidney and the liver, it would be wise to have the function of these two organs checked via creatine clearance (this can be done with a blood test known as a chem screen) before a determination of a healthy amount of dietary protein is made. In an individual with a healthy kidney and liver no research has shown a change in the filtration rate of the kidney associated with a change in dietary protein.

Forty-four grams of protein per day are the recommended amount for the elderly. It is good to note here that the incidence of a condition called protein-energy malnutrition (PEM) is between 35 and 65 percent. This is usually in a subclinical or secondary state and is not symptomatic until a primary or chronic disease occurs. It often accompanies heart, lung, kidney or liver disease, and because of this, it is rarely diagnosed on its own. The most common presenting symptom of PEM is confusion or an altered mental state. Persons who have PEM often also have inadequate fluid intakes. Since the symptoms of dehydration and PEM are so similar and these two problems so often occur together, they are rarely diagnosed individually or even at all. The diagnosis and treatment are usually for the primary or presenting illness rather than these two problems.

Fat

Because of its association with heart disease and obesity, most of us know that fat is to be reduced in our diets. This is true for the elderly, women and people in recovery as well as for the general public. Fats are the most calorie-dense component of our diets. By limiting our intake of fats we are also able to limit our caloric intake without decreasing protein or carbohydrate consumption.

Fluids

Adequate fluid intake is problematic for the elderly. As we age our kidneys age with us, and some kidneys will not be able to concentrate urine as effectively as they did in younger years. This can lead to incontinence. In an attempt to control incontinence people often try to limit their fluid intake. This can lead to dehydration. Dehydration can also be caused by intravenous fluid treatment, flu, diarrhea, vomiting or hemorrhage. It is important to note that caffeine acts as a diuretic. Increasing the amount of coffee you drink each day will not help to keep you better hydrated but will in fact only dehydrate you more. It is important to cut down on the amount of coffee, black tea and soda that you drink and increase your intake of water. Fruit juices are helpful, but they are loaded with fructose, which is a sugar and should be limited. Herbal teas are a good way to maintain a high hydration level.

Suggested Nutritional Supplementation
For Women Over 55

If a woman has been in recovery and sober for several years, the following is good on a daily basis. If she is newly in recovery and has been using alcohol for a number of years, twice this amount can be taken for approximately three to four months without being problematic.

Protein	44 grams/day

Fat Soluble Vitamins

Vitamin A	6000 IU/day
Vitamin D	400 IU/day
Vitamin E	45 IU/day
Vitamin K	15 mcg/day

Water Soluble Vitamins

Vitamin B1	100 mg/day
Vitamin B2	100 mg/day
Vitamin B6	50 mg/day
Vitamin B12	25 mcg/day
Biotin	30 mcg/day
Folic Acid	400 mcg/day
Niacinamide	20 mg/day
Pantothenic Acid	10 mg/day
Vitamin C	500 mg/day

Minerals

Calcium	200 mg/day
Copper	2 mg/day
Magnesium	100 mg/day
Iron	18 mg/day
Iodine	150 mcg/day
Phosphorus	48 mg/day
Zinc	15 mg/day

Chloride	72 mg/day
Chromium	100 mcg/day
Manganese	2.5 mcg/day
Molybdenum	25 mcg/day
Nickel	5 mcg/day
Potassium	80 mg/day
Selenium	25 mcg/day
Silicon	10 mcg/day
Vanadium	10 mcg/day

Fatty Acids

Gamma Linoleic	50 mg/day
Cis Linoleic	50 mg/day

The amount of chromium is higher for older people because persons over the age of 50 tend to have difficulty with sugar metabolism and chromium aids in this process.

500 mg/day of Evening Primrose Oil reduces the craving for alcohol.

Appendix 5

Exercise And The Older Woman

As a woman ages her body often requires extra attention to maintain its flexibility and endurance. Daily stretches or yoga are good flexibility-builders. Stretches done underwater in a swimming pool are a bit easier yet no less effective. Swimming, walking, bike-riding and similar low-impact aerobic exercises support cardiovascular health and promote overall fitness.

A few specific stretches will start your day right or unkink your body after long hours of sitting:

- *A morning stretch.* This helps wake up your body even before you get out of bed. While lying in bed, stretch one arm up and then the other. Push your arms forward while opening your hands wide, then pull your arms back and close your hands. For your legs, pull your knees up toward your midsection, do a few slow bicycle turns, then stretch your legs out straight. This exercise is also good before or after a session of extended exercise.

- **Shoulder circles.** Circle your shoulders backward in a wide arc.
- **Head circles.** Circle your head slowly and gently, first to the left, then to the right.
- **Back arch.** Place your hands in the small of your back and arch gently backward. If you have trouble with an excessively arched back, don't do this exercise. Most people, however, need to arch their backs more than they do. For safety's sake, do these standing up.
- **Upper-body stretch.** Stand in a doorway. Grab both sides of the doorway, with your hands behind you at about shoulder level. Let your arms straighten as you lean forward. Hold your chest up and chin in.
- **Body curl.** Sitting in a chair, lean forward and touch your toes. Unwind and sit back up, allowing your spine to uncurl one vertebra at a time.
- **Leg and foot stretch.** Extend your leg, circle your toes and point your toes. To build strength in your bones and ankles, rotate your feet in the shapes of the letters of the alphabet.

(Adapted from *Everyday Health Tips*, published by *Prevention* Magazine Health Books.)

Bibliography And Suggested Readings

Arcana, Judith. **Our Mothers' Daughters.** Berkeley, CA: Shameless Hussy Press, 1979.

Bierig, Sandra. **Transforming The Co-dependent Woman.** Deerfield Beach, FL: Health Communications, 1991.

Black, Claudia. **Double Duty: Dual Dynamics Within The Chemically Dependent Home.** New York: Ballantine Books, 1990.

De Beauvoir, Simone. **The Second Sex.** Trans. and ed. by H. M. Parshley. New York: Knopf, 1953.

De Rosis, Helen A. **Women And Anxiety.** New York: Delacorte Press, 1979.

Doress, Paula Brown, and Diana Laskin Siegel. **Ourselves, Growing Older: Women Aging With Power And Knowledge.** New York: Touchstone, 1987.

Erikson, Erik H. **Identity: Youth and Crisis.** New York: W. W. Norton, 1968.

Feltman, John, ed. **Prevention's Giant Book Of Health Facts.** Emmaus, PA: Rodale Press, 1991.

Fishel, Ruth. **The Power Of Words** (pamphlet for effective affirmation writing) Deerfield Beach, FL: Health Communications, 1992.

Fishel, Ruth. **Time For Joy.** Daily Affirmations. Deerfield Beach, FL: Health Communications, 1988.

Forward, Susan, and Craig Buck. **Toxic Parents.** New York: Bantam Books, 1989.

Gideon, William L., ed. **Alcoholism Counseling.** 3 vols. Matteson, IL: Good and Golden, 1976.

Grau, Lois, and Ida Susser, eds. **Women in the Later Years: Health, Social, and Cultural Perspectives.** Binghamton, NY: Harrington Park Press, 1989.

Greenspan, Miriam. **A New Approach to Women And Therapy.** New York: McGraw-Hill, 1985.

Hay, Louise L. **You Can Heal Your Life.** Santa Monica, CA: Hay House, 1987.

Hoffman, Virginia. **Birthing A Living Church.** New York: Crossroads Publishing, 1988.

Howard, Doris, ed. **The Dynamics Of Feminist Therapy.** New York: Haworth Press, 1986.

Janeway, Elizabeth. **Between Myth And Morning: Women Awakening.** New York: William Morrow, 1975.

Larsen, Earnie. **Stage II Recovery: Life Beyond Addiction.** San Francisco: Harper and Row, 1985.

Lerner, Harriet Goldhor. **The Dance Of Anger.** New York: Perennial Library, 1989.

Macdonald, Barbara, and Cynthia Rich. **Look Me in the Eye: Old Women, Aging and Ageism.** San Francisco: Spinsters/Aunt Lute, 1983.

Mansmann, Patricia A., and Patricia A. Neuhausel. **Life After Survival.** 2nd rev. ed. Malvern, PA: Genesis Publishing, 1989.

Mariechild, Diane. **Mother Wit.** rev. ed. Trumansburg, NY: The Crossing Press, 1989.

Mueller, L. Ann, and Katherine Ketcham. **Recovery: How To Get And Stay Sober.** New York: Bantam, 1987.

Nierenberg, Gerard I. **Women And The Art Of Negotiating.** New York: Fireside Books, 1985.

Rich, Adrienne. **On Lies, Secrets, And Silence.** New York: W. W. Norton, 1979.

Sandmaier, Marian. **The Invisible Alcoholics.** New York: McGraw-Hill, 1981.

Sanford, Linda Tschirhart, and Mary Ellen Donovan. **Women and Self-Esteem.** New York: Penguin Books, 1984.

Schaef, Anne Wilson. **Women's Reality.** Minneapolis: Winston Press, 1981.

Sheppard, Alice. "From Kate Sanborn To Feminist Psychology: The Social Context Of Women's Humor, 1885-1985." *Psychology of Women Quarterly* 10 (June 1986), 155–70.

Small, Jacquelyn. **Becoming Naturally Therapeutic.** rev. ed. New York: Bantam, 1990.

Smith, Ann W. **Overcoming Perfectionism.** Deerfield Beach, FL: Health Communications, 1990.

Stephenson, June. **Women's Roots: Status And Achievements In Western Civilization.** 3rd ed. Napa, CA: Diemer-Smith Publishing, 1988.

Valley-Fox, Anne, and Sam Keen. **Your Mythic Journey.** Los Angeles: J. P. Tarcher, 1989.

Wegscheider-Cruse, Sharon. **Another Chance.** Palo Alto, CA: Science and Behavior Books, 1981.

Whitfield, Charles L. **Healing The Child Within.** Pompano Beach, FL: Health Communications, 1987.

The Witches Cave. A play written by five French Canadian feminist women in the 1970s.

I leave my heart behind — I feel the loss / the intensity of the connection / the ?? of it ——— the peacefulness & the completeness of the connection — that